Toronto Dance Theatre
1968–1998
Stages in a Journey

Nadine Saxton

Katherine Cornell

Captus Press

Toronto Dance Theatre 1968–1998
Stages in a Journey

© 1998 by Captus Press and the authors

Canadian Cataloguing in Publication Data

Saxton, Nadine, 1961–
  Toronto Dance Theatre 1968–1998: stages in a journey

Includes bibliographical references and index.
ISBN 1–895712–21–1

1. Toronto Dance Theatre — History.
I. Cornell, Katherine, 1972–   .
II. Title.

GV1786.T665S29 1998   792.8'09713'541   C98–932612–8

Captus Press Inc.
Mail: York University Campus
        4700 Keele Street
        North York, Ontario
        M3J 1P3
Telephone: (416) 736–5537
Fax: (416) 736–5793
Email: Info@captus.com
Website: http://www.captus.com

0 9 8 7 6 5 4 3 2 1
Printed in Canada

*For Christopher, Alexander,
Judy, Jack and Joan*

and

*For my Grandmothers, Mona
and Betty*

The research for this book was made
possible, in part, by a grant from the
Office of Research, York University.
A special grant from private sources
helped ensure its publication.

Table of Contents

THIS BOOK IS A LOVE STORY. In the style of those monumental novels that chronicle the span of generations, the story of Toronto Dance Theatre is a saga of grand passions and epic lives. It is an eventful history driven by genius. And by lunacy, by inspiration, high ambitions, love, camaraderie, struggle, jealousy, betrayal, by bold creations, great achievements, and by the endless hard work and deep beauty of dance.

Toronto Dance Theatre was founded by three extraordinary individuals: Peter Randazzo, Patricia Beatty, and David Earle. The order of their names, and it never varied, reveals a great deal about who they are and how they functioned together. Peter had performed in Martha Graham's company, a dancer of tremendous even frightening intensity with a personality that demanded room and attention; he was not so much a leader as a

Foreword . . .

Peggy Baker
Toronto, June 1998

force. Trish was the fulcrum, in possession of a striking, sensual, female energy, working quietly from the inside out, slow, sure, intuitive, ready to share. David's deep spiritual commitment to a life in art and the value he placed on humility in the face of the awesome nature of creation, made him oblivious to any considerations of hierarchy. In a rare dance world alliance, Pete, Trish, and Dave joined forces to create a dance company and dedicated it by name to the city that would be the home for their life's work.

TDT arrived in Toronto in a blaze of glory and was championed in the press for a time. The dancers were revered as cult heroes by adoring fans. The city has been, by turns, excitable, proud, uncomprehending, appreciative, inattentive, fascinated, disdainful, overwhelmed. David summed it up at one point in his infamous statement [at the Toronto Arts Awards] "for twenty years we've been making love to Toronto and for twenty years Toronto has had a headache."

This book chronicles the heady ups and vertiginous downs, the tragedies, comedies, and dramas that unfolded in the studios, offices, and theatres where Toronto Dance Theatre engaged in its daily life. I am a bit player in this big story. I enter in and pass through with a multitude of others, but the interaction brought me to my own life's work and to the heart of myself.

I met Patricia Beatty in 1968 at a summer theatre school in Alberta where she had been brought in to teach movement for actors. She was a breathtaking beauty, thin as a reed with long dark hair, a 32-year-old dancer fresh from New York City. I was a very young 16-year-old from the suburbs of Edmonton and I spent those few weeks of classes in a state of rapture. Trish taught us to dance sitting and rolling on the floor. Her torso and limbs curving, twisting, arching, coiling, and exploding. She swayed and billowed, pressed, pushed, pierced, dug, scooped. She spoke like a poet about earth, weight, the roots and trunks and limbs of trees, the cycling of seasons, the shifts of the heart. She instructed us to plié in second with the bearing of a Chinese Emperor, to lift our arms as though they carried a weight of heavy fabric, or to hold them as if they rested on the arms of a huge chair, to turn our heads with a terrible truth held in our chest, to dig furrows with the plow blades of our heels. And the seed of every movement defined in this endless stream of images needed to find its beginning in the core of our bodies: the spine and the pelvis. I was being introduced to the technique of Martha Graham, and I was being taught by a great artist. In dance I discovered the language in which I am most fluent, eloquent and connected and that discovery catapulted me into my future.

In 1971, I came to Toronto to study full time with TDT. I took classes in the same studios where the dancers of the company, who were my teachers, trained and rehearsed. The ritual for beginning class distills the essence of the learning we undertook. Before the class started, students lounged on the floor chatting, stretching, limbering up, perhaps reviewing an exercise from a previous class. The musician might be tuning congas or noodling on the piano. When the teacher arrived in the room there was quiet and all of the dancers stood up and took a place. We focused on the teacher who stood front and centre and in this stillness, each of us — students, teacher, and accompanist — silently put aside all other concerns and committed ourselves to the task ahead. In that moment was held a sense of mutual respect for the work and one another. The teacher sat down at the front of the studio facing the students, legs bent diamond-wise, soles of feet together. Then the students sat, mirroring the teacher. A single word was spoken, "and." Every head bowed into the first exercise and the musician met us with the perfect tempo and rhythm. Class was always intense, uplifting, and invigorating. It could also be austere or brimming with emotion. I remember in one of my first classes, David Earle jarred the class by stopping in the middle of an exercise. He looked directly at me and softly declared that a dancer never attended to their hair touching it or tossing it back, while they were dancing. I was flushed with shame, but it was a great lesson in discipline and commitment; the pressure of the moment in dance must never be interrupted by a trivial gesture.

Although I did my first professional performances as an apprentice with Toronto Dance Theatre and made my first trip abroad with the company, my own path as a dancer led elsewhere, and I never became a member of that gorgeous group as I had dreamed I might. It has been my pleasure, though, to know those artists and to watch them and to continue to learn from them and the generations that have followed. The dances and the dancing cannot be held in a book. But the history contained here offers a rare glimpse into the realm of purposeful immediacy that Martha Graham called "a dancer's world." The story of TDT is big and complex, beautiful and inspiring with a strain of sadness: a love story.

Canadian Modern Dance

There have been pioneers in the modern dance in
Canada. Many were of European origin and had
studied the techniques of the German modern danc-
ers Mary Wigman, Rudolf von Laban and Hanya
Holm. In Toronto Bianca Rogge, Yoné Kvietys and
Nancy Lima Dent all had companies in Canadian
Dance Festivals. There they were joined by the
Montreal choreographers such as Elizabeth Leese,
Jeanne Renaud and Berouthé Nagys, whose
work has born fruit in many companies such as
Le Groupe de la Place Royale, Le Groupe de
la Nouvel' Aire and the Contemporary Dance
Theatre of Hugo Romero.

In western Canada a flowering of
modern dance is now in progress. There
are professional companies in most of
the western capitals, notably Contemporary Dancers in Winnipeg, directed
by Rachel Browne, and the Anna
Wyman Dance Theatre in Vancouver.

Toronto Dance Theatre
1974 Souvenir Programme

For many Canadians, the
founding of Toronto Dance
Theatre signalled the beginning of modern dance in
Canada. The gracious ack-
nowledgment by the found-
ers of TDT that modern
dance was already a
presence in Canada
before they arrived
on the scene, sets
an honourable pre-
cedent for us.

First, we ex-
press our deep

Preface

thanks to Peter, Trish, David, and Christopher. They have supported us throughout the entire research and writing with patience and a great sensitivity for our own creative process. Next, we acknowledge the help of Peggy Baker. She did so much more than just write our Foreword. Her words and constant encouragement guided us through TDT's epic and complex story.

This book has been seven years in the making. The background history was researched and developed for Nadine's MA thesis, *Toronto Dance Theatre: An Example of Arts Administration in Canada*. In 1998, Kate, archivist for TDT in 1997 and 1998, curated an exhibition of archival material from the TDT at the IDA Gallery at York University. The photos and the stories that came from both the exhibit and the thesis, were an irresistible invitation to celebrate a unique history. Interviewees from the thesis project were contacted and consent to use their words was granted. Thank you, James Plaxton, Roger Jones, Ed Oscapella, the late Ken Pierson, and Ellen Busby. Along with the founders, Christopher, and Peggy, we also interviewed friends and dancers, past and present. Donald Himes, Rosemary James, Karen duPlessis, Suzette Sherman, Denis Joffre, Michael Trent, Susan Macpherson, Ahmed Hassan, Kenny Pearl, Jini Stolk, Coralee McLaren, and Ron Snippe were generous with their time and interest. Others who shared their memories and experiences were the late Gladys Forrester, Susan Cash, Holly Small, Graham McKelvie, Karen Bowes-Sewell, Penny Olorenshaw, Billyann Balay, Terrill Maguire, Lawrence and Miriam Adams, Luc Tremblay, Carolyn Gossage, and Martin and Judy Hunter. Thank you all. We know that there were so many others we could have interviewed and we hope that they will recognize their part through the stories we have chosen to tell.

Graham Jackson's articles, essays and reviews on TDT (published and unpublished) were touchstones and guides for us. His insight into the complex relationships inherent in the creative process, and his understanding of the totality of the work and its impact on those that were present to witness it, gave us the lens, both close and wide-angled, through which to view the journey.

Many institutions supplied us with information for this book and we thank the entire staff at Toronto Dance Theatre, especially Jini, Heather, Claire, Victoria, Carla, and Michael. The York University Archives and Special Collections houses the TDT collection and has been an invaluable resource. We thank the archivists at the

National Ballet Archives and Bennington College, who spent countless hours searching for just the right photograph. We would also like to thank Keith Cornell for his artistic help with all the visual elements and Juliana Saxton, whose editorial experience and memories of Toronto in the sixties and seventies have added so much to this book.

There were many people behind the scenes who helped us: our transcribers, Sarala Dandekar and Colleen Lowey; Carol Creasy who lent us her computer at a critical moment; the folks at Now Café who let us use their space as an unofficial office; and Bridget Cauthery who put Kate on the path.

For those who work behind the scenes in theatre, the criterion of their success is that they remain invisible and so their companionship and their contributions have only received passing mention. We want to acknowledge them here. Without the tireless commitment and creative energies of these silent partners, the productions wouldn't have happened, the performances never have taken place.

Lastly, we would like individually, to thank our friends and families who, times beyond count, allowed us the freedom from responsibilities and duties that should have been ours. We are more grateful than they can ever know for their love and support and concern for our well-being. We missed you, too.

The body spiral is in many ways the core of the Graham technique. For us, it is the metaphor that embodies the history of Toronto Dance Theatre and the extraordinary passion which drives dance artists to create again and again. The story of TDT is one of revolving cycles of energy and during those cycles, it has been the particular passion of individuals that has impelled the spiral. We want to honour that passion and the lives of those who engage their whole selves in the search for their own truth which lies, of course, in the body of their work.

Many people asked us, "Are you going to tell the truth?" Each one has his or her own version of "the truth." This is ours, as close as we can make it.

Photo Credits

Every effort was made to identify and contact the copyright holders for the photographs in this book. Upon notification, any credits will be corrected in subsequent editions. The authors would like to thank all those listed below who generously lent us personal photographs to enhance the visual scope of the book. All the other photographs come courtesy of Toronto Dance Theatre.

1. Front cover: The Company in *Sacra Conversazione*, Miriane Braaf, Rosemary James, Suzette Sherman, Christopher House, Crispin Redhead, Coralee McLaren, Monica Burr, Laurence Lemieux, Graham McKelvie, Sean Marye, Kate Alton, Pascal Desrosiers, and David Pressault. Choreographer: David Earle; Photographer: Cylla von Tiedemann; Costume Designer: Denis Joffre.

2. Page i: Peter Randazzo, Christopher House, Patricia Beatty, and David Earle. Photographer: Cylla von Tiedemann.

3. Page ix: Peggy Baker as a young apprentice circa 1973. Photographer: Jake Peters.

4. Page 2: Lilian Jarvis, principal dancer with the National Ballet and friend of the founders circa the late 1950s. Photographer: Ken Bell; photograph courtesy of the National Ballet of Canada Archives.

5. Page 3: Patricia at about age 4, photographs courtesy of Patricia Beatty.

6. Page 4: Trish Beatty in 1955 at Bennington College. Photographer: Unknown; photograph courtesy of Bennington College Archives.

7. Page 8: Trish in *First Music*. Choreographer: Patricia Beatty; Photographer: Unknown; Costume Designers: Denis Joffre and Susan Macpherson; photograph courtesy of David Earle.

8. Page 10: David Earle and Trish Beatty talking in the foreground, with Amelia Itcush rehearsing in the background. Photographer: Unknown; photograph courtesy of CBC Studios.

9. Page 11: Portrait of David Earle circa 1960; photograph courtesy of Donald Himes.

10. Page 12: David Earle, co-founder. Photographer: Unknown.

11. Page 15: Peter Randazzo and David Earle on vacation in Eastern Ontario; photograph courtesy of Donald Himes.

12. Page 21: A young David Earle and Peter Randazzo; photograph courtesy of Donald Himes.

13. Page 24: TDT's first programme from December 1968, courtesy of Toronto Dance Theatre Archives, York University.

14. Page 27: Claudia Moore and Chuck Flanders in *Angelic Visitation #1*. Choreographer: David Earle; Photographer: Andrew Oxenham, Costume Designer: Norberto Chiesa.

15. Page 28: Celia Franca and James Ronaldson in the National Ballet's production of *Lilac Garden*. Choreographer: Antony Tudor; Photographer: Ken Bell; photograph courtesy of the National Ballet of Canada Archives.

16. Page 28: Peter Randazzo and Amelia Itcush in *Encounter*. Choreographer: Peter Randazzo; Photographer: Unknown; Costume Designer: Susan Macpherson.

17. Page 29: *Against Sleep* is one of Trish's early signature works; here she dances with co-founder David Earle. Choreographer: Patricia Beatty; Photographer: Rudi Christl; Costume Designer: Susan Macpherson.

18. Page 30: The young company on tour. Photographer: Unknown; photograph courtesy of David Earle.

19. Page 34: Flyer from TDT's first visit to England in 1972, courtesy of Toronto Dance Theatre Archives, York University.

20. Page 35: Patricia in *Rhapsody in the Late Afternoon*. Choreographer: Patricia Beatty; Photographer: Unknown; Costume Designer: Susan Macpherson.

21. Page 36: David Earle, Merle Salsberg, Peter Randazzo, and Patricia Beatty crossing the channel to France in April 1972. Photographer: Unknown.

22. Page 37: Three young dancers with high cheekbones, Kathy Wildberger, Patricia Beatty, and Amelia Itcush, circa 1971. Photographer: Unknown.

23. Page 38: Flyer from TDT's fourth season at Toronto Workshop Productions, courtesy Toronto Dance Theatre Archives, York University.

24. Page 39: Barry Smith in *Starscape*. Choreographer: Peter Randazzo; Photographer: Unknown; Costume Designer: Susan Macpherson.

25. Page 40: Keith Urban, Barry Smith, Merle Salsberg, and Susan Macpherson from the film portion of *Operetta*.

Choreographer: David Earle; Photographer: Ken Mimura; Costume Designer: Ken Mimura.

26. Page 41: Nancy Ferguson and Ricardo Abreut in *Rhapsody in the Late Afternoon*. Choreographer: Patricia Beatty, Photographer: Andrew Oxenham; Costume Designer: Susan Macpherson.

27. Page 42: The company in *Atlantis* circa 1973–74, Kathryn Brown, Barry Smith, Sara Pettitt, Patricia Beatty, Danny Grossman, David Wood, Ricardo Abreut, Susan Macpherson, Helen Jones, Norrey Drummond, Patricia Miner, John Preston, Merle Salsberg, Cornelius Fisher-Credo, and Peggy Baker. Choreographer: David Earle; Photographer: Unknown; Costume Designer: Astrid Janson.

28. Page 43: Barry Smith, Danny Grossman, David Wood, Norrey Drummond, Kathryn Brown, and Merle Salsberg in "Hit the Road Jack" from *Ray Charles Suite*. Choreographer: David Earle; Photographer: Unknown; Costume Designer: Astrid Janson.

29. Page 44: Trish with David Wood, as a GO Train commuter, in *Harold Morgan's Delicate Balance*. Choreographer: Patricia Beatty; Photographer: David Davis; Costume Designer: Astrid Janson.

30. Page 45: *Babar — The Little Elephant*. Choreographer: Donald Himes; Photographer: Andrew Oxenham; Costume Designer: Peggy Wasman.

31. Page 46: David with *Babar* choreographer Donald Himes; photograph courtesy of Donald Himes.

32. Page 51: Enter Dr. Roger Jones, general manager. Photographer: Jake Peters.

33. Page 56: Barry Smith in *Boat, River, Moon*, one of the pieces performed at Sadler's Wells Theatre. Choreographer: David Earle; Photographer: David Davis; Costume Designer: Astrid Janson.

34. Page 58: Revival of *Nighthawks*, featuring Almond Small, Sean Marye, Christopher House, Laurence Lemieux, and Suzette Sherman. Choreographer: Peter Randazzo; Photographer: Andrew Oxenham; Costume Designer: Carol Crawley.

35. Page 58: *L'Assassin Menace*. Choreographer: Peter Randazzo; Photographer: Unknown; Costume Designer: Carol Crawley.

36. Page 60: The exquisite Claudia Moore in *Mythos*. Choreographer: David Earle; Photographer: Rudi Christl; Costume Designer: Carol Crawley.

37. Page 60: Dennis René Highway in *Mythos*. Choreographer: David Earle; Photographer: Frank Richards; Costume Designer: Carol Crawley.

38. Page 61: Patricia Beatty, Lois Smith, former principal dancer with the National Ballet, Bill Orlowski, founder of the National Tap Dance Company, and Danny Grossman at a reception. Photographer: Andrew Oxenham.

39. Page 62: The company in *National Spirit*. Choreographer: Danny Grossman; Photographer: Andrew Oxenham; Costume Designer: Mary Kerr.

40. Page 63: Chuck Flanders, one of the new company members, in his birthday suit. Photographer unknown; photograph courtesy of David Earle.

41. Page 68: 80 Winchester Street in Cabbagetown, the new home of TDT. Photographer: Kate Cornell.

42. Page 69: The 10th anniversary programme at the Royal Alexandra Theatre included *Recital*, featuring Claudia Moore, Chuck Flanders, Sherry Lanier, Robert Desrosiers, and Nancy Ferguson. Choreographer: Peter Randazzo; Photographer: Andrew Oxenham; Costume Designer: Carol Crawley.

43. Page 72: The company at ease, taken from 1979 flyer. From left to right Christopher House, Nancy Ferguson, David Earle, Robert Desrosiers, Dennis René Highway, Suzette Sherman, Claudia Moore, Sherri Lanier, Susan Macpherson, Karen duPlessis, Jeannie Teillet, Patricia Beatty, Grace Miyagawa, Chuck Flanders, Peter Randazzo, Wendy Chiles, Mitch Kirsch, and Sara Pettitt. Photographer: Unknown; courtesy of Toronto Dance Theatre Archives, York University.

44. Page 73: Susan Macpherson in a studio shot. After TDT she would go on to become a noted independent choreographer and teacher. Photographer: Frank Richards.

45. Page 75: Trish in *Lessons in Another Language*. Choreographer: Patricia Beatty; Photographer: Andrew Oxenham, Costume Designer: Evelyn Bastien.

46. Page 76: The company in *Baroque Suite* circa 1981. Choreographer: David Earle; Photographer: Andrew Oxenham; Costume Designer: Astrid Janson.

47. Page 81: The new general manager, Ed Oscapella. Photographer: Unknown; photograph from *Dance Ontario News/Quarterly*, circa 1981.

48. Page 84: Kenny Pearl dancing with the Alvin Ailey American Dance Theater in *Revelations*. Choreographer: Alvin Ailey; Photographer: Unknown; photograph courtesy of Kenny Pearl.

49. Page 89: Christopher House, the new resident choreographer, with Karen duPlessis in *Animated Shorts*. Choreographer: Christopher House; Photographer: Frank Richards; Costume Designer: Denis Joffre.

50. Page 89: Denis Joffre's costume design for a female dancer in *Glass Houses*. Choreographer: Christopher House; courtesy of Denis Joffre.

51. Page 90: Sara Pettitt in *Enter the Dawn*, choreography inspired by Edward Hopper's painting. Choreographer: Peter Randazzo; Photographer: Andrew Oxenham; Costume Designer: Denis Joffre.

52. Page 91: The company performing in *Raptures and Ravings* from *Painters in the Dance*. Choreographer: Patricia Beatty; Photographer: Andrew Oxenham; Costume Designer: Denis Joffre.

53. Page 94: The inmates from the Second Act of *Court of Miracles*. Conceived by David Earle; Photographer: Unknown; Costume Designers: Denis Joffre and Susan Rome.

54. Page 95: Learie McNicolls, Lisa Bunsey, Gillian Ferrabee, and Karen duPlessis as the Animals in *Court of Miracles*. Conceived by David Earle; Photographer: Unknown; Costume Designers: Denis Joffre and Susan Rome.

55. Page 90: The company in *Sacra Conversazione*. Choreographer: David Earle; Photographer: Unknown; Costume Designer: Denis Joffre.

56. Page 96: The staff assuming the Sacra pose, Ricardo Abreut, Sheenah Andrews, Billyann Balay, Ellen Bubsy, Jennifer Dick, Tanya Lockyer, Dawn Masters, Jill Palmer, Victoria Thompson, Ron Ward, and Angelica Willkie. Photographer: Unknown.

57. Page 99: David Earle. Photographer: Unknown.

58. Page 100: The late executive director, Ken Pierson. Photographer: Cylla von Tiedemann.

59. Page 101: A poster for the School of Toronto Dance Theatre prepared before they travelled to Aberdeen Scotland in 1988. Photographer: Unknown; courtesy of Toronto Dance Theatre Archives, York University.

60. Page 103: Denis Joffre's costume design for Christopher House's *green evening, warm and clear*, courtesy of Denis Joffre.

61. Page 104: The joyous *Handel Variations* remains one of Christopher's most popular works; the photograph features Christopher House, Suzette Sherman, and Sean Marye. Choreographer: Christopher House; Photographer: Cylla von Tiedemann; Costume Designer: Denis Joffre.

Photographer: Cylla von Tiedemann; Wardrobe Co-ordinator: Lori McLean.

75. Page 118: David Earle and Suzette Sherman, master and muse performing together. Photographer: Cylla von Tiedemann; photograph courtesy of Suzette Sherman.

76. Page 123: David Earle and Helen Jones in *Schola Cantorum*. Choreographer: Christopher House; Photographer: Andrew Oxenham; Costume Designer: Audrey Vanderstoop; photograph courtesy of Christopher House.

77. Page 124: Christopher House in his solo work *Schubert Dances*, which he performed while with Les Grands Ballets Canadiens. Choreographer: Christopher House; Photographer: Cylla von Tiedemann; Costume Designer: Denis Joffre; photograph courtesy of Christopher House.

78. Page 125: Jini Stolk became general manager in 1994. Photographer: David Leyes.

79. Page 130. Sasha Ivanochko in performance of *Book of Hours*. Choreographer: Christopher House; Photographer: Unknown; Costume Designer: Jane Townsend; photograph courtesy of Christopher House.

80. Page 130: The company in *Pingo Slink*. Choreographer: Christopher House; Photographer: Cylla von Tiedemann; Costume Designer: Jane Townsend.

81. Page 131: Ron Stewart in *Apollo's Touch*. Choreographer: Christopher House; Photographer: Cylla von Tiedemann; Costume Designer: Jane Townsend.

82. Page 131: The collaborators: Michael J. Baker, composer with Arraymusic, Peggy Baker, independent artist, and Christopher House, artistic director. Photographer: Unknown; photograph courtesy of Christopher House.

83. Page 131: Laurence Lemieux in her Dora Award winning performance of *Cryptoversa*. Choreographer: Christopher House; Photographer: Cylla von Tiedemann; Wardrobe Co-ordinator: Lori McLean.

84. Page 138: David teaching company class at the "Y". Photographer: Unknown.

85. Page 140: Peter Randazzo at ease for a promotional photo, "The Great Days." Photographer: Louis Falco; flyer courtesy of Toronto Dance Theatre Archives, York University.

86. Page 145: Ron Snippe, lighting designer and long standing member of the company. Photographer: Unknown.

87. Page 145: Karen duPlessis and Christopher House partnered in *Boulevard*. Choreographer: Christopher House; Photographer: Andrew Oxenham; Costume Designer: Denis Joffre.

1 TORONTO DANCE THEATRE was officially launched in 1968, marking the beginning of an extended working relationship between Patricia (Trish) Beatty, David Earle, and Peter Randazzo. Prior to the founding of the company, the lives of these three people would intersect a number of times and in a number of places.

For most Canadians in the early sixties, modern dance, like much of the "modern" arts, fell within the pejorative "creative" or, more bluntly, "that artsy-fartsy stuff." Young Canadian artists who had an interest in exploring freer, emotionally and spiritually centred expressive movement went off to study at the Martha Graham School of Contemporary Dance in New York City. There they received a rigorous and demanding training from Miss Graham herself and her company dancers. The Graham technique was not, however, about skill acquisition. It was a ritual act, a preparation of the soul for understanding and enlightenment. "It is," says Peggy Baker, "a way of communicating that gives dignity ... it gave being a dance student in class a profound meaning ... a place to attach spiritual values."

Peter Randazzo, an American, a dancer with the Martha Graham Dance Company at this time, and a class demonstrator at the school, had already introduced himself to

"If we can't do what we want, we might as well work at Woolworth's."

Trish Beatty, 1969

Canadian David Earle. Both men remember seeing Patricia Beatty, who was also taking classes at the Graham Studios. Neither could believe that she was Canadian. Peter, because Trish was so unlike any Canadian he had ever met, was convinced that her parents "must own a bowling alley in Brooklyn." David, at his first sight of Trish in "purple tights and a purple leotard," remembers thinking she was "too visible" to be a Canadian. The formal introduction of the future artistic triumvirate did not take place until 1967.

That year was a watershed for the arts in Canada. The celebration of 100 years of nationhood, provided an opportunity for the federal government to give, through generous financial grants, a kind of public seal of approval of the arts as legitimate pursuits for its citizenry. While "modern" dance may not have been quite what the government had in mind, its promotion of the arts as national currencies at Expo 67 generated an atmosphere of curiosity, discovery, and broadened horizons.

Looking back through the years, unreliable memory tends to fade the sequence of introductions and events, but it seems that Lilian Jarvis, a former dancer with the National Ballet of Canada and herself a student of Graham, was the connection among the three founders. Randazzo and Beatty speculate that they all met in Toronto at the home of Donald Himes, who operated as an informal drop-in centre for Toronto's burgeoning "non-traditional" dance community. Their meeting was inevitable. As Trish Beatty explains, "Every modern dancer knew each other in the city. There were only about eleven of us." Apart from the specifics of the initial sightings and a more receptive cultural atmosphere, the background of each of the founders is an important element in understanding and celebrating the establishment of Toronto

Dance Theatre and the growth of modern dance in Canada.

Patricia (Trish) Beatty

Trish Beatty was born on 13 May 1936 in Toronto. "I was born to save my mother's life. She had a chemical imbalance in her system and the doctors told her to get well she should have another baby." This "therapeutic" child of an affluent family grew up in Forest Hill and attended Havergal College, a private girls' school. The youngest of four children, Trish had a strong and independent spirit; she was energetic and athletic and certainly did not fit the mold of the quiet, good little girl of that period. "I felt more than this 'good little girl.' I was six and I saw that my brothers were having a lot more fun than my sister, so I thought, 'I'm going with them'." Her first experience in dance was at eight with Jean McPherson. "She had us all flying around like butterflies in the Heliconian Club." At nine, her parents, seeing the need for more structure, enrolled her in ballet classes with Gladys Forrester. She "ignited a spirit in me that still continues today." In 1950, Forrester had joined Gweneth Lloyd (co-founder of the Royal Winnipeg Ballet)

as her assistant when Miss Lloyd opened a school at 719 Yonge Street in Toronto. Forrester remembers Trish as being "a lovely mover, she had great expression; she had great soul and a good sense of humour." In 1998, Gladys recalled: "Trish was studying for a Royal Academy of Dancing exam. I said, 'Trish, if you don't get Honours, I'll eat my hat.' Well, of course, she got Honours and afterwards she brought me a top hat filled with candy anyway and said, Now, you can eat your hat!' "

Trish wanted more from life and dance than ballet had to offer. "I knew I didn't belong in classical dance. My body had more appetite than the positions ballet would allow. I was an athlete and wanted a feeling of physical power and real freedom. Ballet wasn't sensuous enough for me. Miss Lloyd was the only one I knew who'd heard about modern dance.... Her sense of dance was so pure." Lloyd encouraged Trish to go to the United States to find out about modern dance and, in 1955, after graduating from Havergal, Trish went off to Bennington College in Vermont where it was possible to major in choreography and performance in modern dance.

At Bennington, the discovery of modern dance changed her life. She was given the courage to assert herself and taught to focus her energy. The creative atmosphere at Bennington and her teachers, Bill Bales in particular, greatly influenced Beatty and her approach to choreography. In her book *Form Without Formula*, she writes, "My teachers put me through a tough verbal examination of what, why, and for how long, before I started a new piece." As part of Bennington's holistic approach to learning, the degree required students to become familiar with the day-to-day operations of a dance company. Beatty chose to spend Bennington's ten-week work term in Toronto working with the National Ballet of Canada where she observed the operation of the company (then in its fourth year) and acted as a "general girl

Friday." It was here that Trish first met Lilian Jarvis who was later to be Trish's catalyst for returning to Canada.

After graduating with a BA from Bennington in 1959, Trish spent some time training with other teachers in New York City before joining the Martha Graham School of Contemporary Dance the following year. She stayed until 1965. During this period, she performed with the company of Lucas Hoving, a founding member of the José Limón Company. She also worked with the companies of Mary Anthony, Sophie Maslow, and Pearl Lang, all of whom had been disciples of Martha Graham during Graham's formative years. It was the experience of working with Pearl Lang that had a great influence on Trish's later contributions to Toronto Dance Theatre.

Pearl Lang's style of movement suited Beatty's body. "She used her torso in what I believe to be a more lyrical and ecstatic way than the traditional way of Martha." It was Lang's strength of character, the depth of her soul, and quality of movement that impressed Beatty. "Pearl was the artistic daughter of Martha's rich work." Trish joined Lang's company and eventually became Lang's teaching and rehearsal assistant both at the Connecticut College School of Dance and at the Juilliard School of Music and Dance. Since dancers did not make much money, Trish also supported herself by teaching creative dance.

> I was unorthodox when it came to teaching children because I didn't have the formal pedagogy. I taught more as a performer to entrance the children ... people wanted me to write children's books because of what I was saying. I realize what I was doing was tapping into a creative source. Kids are a challenge. I remember being asked at the Scarborough School, "Where did I get my training?" I'd say, "The Scarborough School!" What I gave these children is what I lacked in my own early years. I did [this teaching for] the six years I was in New York.

Trish was with Pearl Lang while she was studying with Martha Graham the same five years which "made Graham's work all make sense." Working with Pearl was also a challenge, "You were a war veteran. She had a strong point of view, she was definitely the Goddess Kali version of choreographer." Lang demanded absolute dedication to the art from those around her; she expected the kind of dedication she herself had given to Martha Graham. Trish's already strong and passionate nature was thriving through her relationships with strong passionate artists. In the future, her intensity could be overwhelming for some.

While working with Lang in New York, Beatty became reacquainted with Lilian Jarvis. Jarvis had received one of the first Canada Council grants to study at the Graham School in order to introduce the Graham technique into the curriculum of the National Ballet School of Canada where she was now teaching. In New York, the two women had many conversations plotting the possibilities of bringing the Graham technique to Toronto. Unbeknownst to Trish, Lilian was holding similar conversations with other Canadians at the Graham School.

In 1965, Jarvis invited Beatty to return to Toronto as her technique demonstrator at the National Ballet School. Knowing that the salary would not be sufficient, Lilian arranged other teaching positions for her. According to Trish, Jarvis said, "I have found another place for you to teach, up at the Hebrew 'Y' at Finch. We can't call it modern *dance* because nobody knows what it means. We have to call it modern *jazz*." In those first classes at the "Y," Trish taught a Graham class, then turned on a record player to teach what she hoped was "a jazz combination" before she "sent people home." It seemed to work and her students didn't complain.

After six years in New York, Beatty's education, training, and professional experience both as a dancer and as a teacher provided her with all the tools she needed for her future work as a pioneer of modern dance in Canada, and she couldn't wait to begin. In the year of her return, she was already looking for space to open her own studio. She knew that the Graham technique could only be taught to adults and serious students and Trish was no stranger to the economic realities of a life in dance. She also knew from her earlier successful experiences teaching creative dance to children that this was a viable way to support the enterprise. She understood the benefits of establishing a school to train dancers: not only did it provide the base from which to draw her future company, but it, too, would provide a source of income. Beatty subscribed to Pearl Lang's philosophy that "artists need enough money to have their dignity." For

Beatty as for Lang, money was necessary but always secondary to the work. She made ends meet by teaching for her friend and fellow modern dance teacher, Nadia Pavlychenko, when she was pregnant with her second child, giving creative movement classes for children, and operating her own school.

One of the many people she approached about studio space was Ed Mirvish, a patron of the arts and owner of Honest Ed's, a giant discount department store. Mirvish seemed quite excited about the prospect of building her a studio of glass on top of one of his buildings. Somehow, this type of studio did not sit well with Beatty, "Can you imagine? Glass changing rooms!"

In 1966, she found what she was looking for at 22 Cumberland Street in Yorkville, an area of Toronto just north of a main shopping district and well situated in terms of public transportation. It was above an auto body shop; "My brother's always called it Trish's bawdy shop." The brave few who wanted to learn the Graham style of modern dance found their way to Beatty's studio. These dedicated regular students, who had followed her from studio space to studio space during the past year, were drawn from the Pavlychenko group, the University of Toronto physical education service classes (taught by Yoné Kvietys), and students who had been rejected by the National Ballet School or were unhappy there. Many of her students paid what they could when they could and this pattern of payment carried over into the future.

In that same year, Trish established her own company, the New Dance Group of Canada, drawing from the few people in Toronto that knew about modern dance: Donald Himes, Kevin McGarrigle, Lilian Jarvis, a visiting David Earle, and her small pool of students. She explains how she managed to obtain funding to float and sustain the company:

> My family were a little awkward about me; they weren't ambitious for me at all. I mean, they were like, "Modern Dance! What is that?" I'm a strong willed woman. I knew Toronto was ready [for a modern dance company]. It was a good place because there was money here. I knew people with money and I wasn't scared of them. I sat on their laps when I was a little girl, so I can talk to them. I'm a Taurus; I'm practical; I know that the money has to be there. I often felt

that I knew how to spend it better than other people. So it turns out, I was pretty good at fund-raising. Also, I know what it's like being asked for money, so I think I know how to treat people when asking.

Trish's skills as a fund-raiser would prove valuable in the future.

The New Dance Group of Canada was active between 1966 and 1968. It had a six-member board of directors and, in its lifetime, two company managers. Responding to a letter from Jillian Officer in 1982, Beatty explained that the company was a "modern dance repertory company" whose goal was to "develop dance in the Toronto area as a serious contemporary art form." The training would be based on the Martha Graham technique of dance; choreography would be by the artistic director and "other choreographers of her choice." In the same letter, Beatty encapsulates the history of the New Dance Group's activities:

> The first performing work for the company was a television series for the Anglican Church based on the themes of Love, Work, and Leisure. The most memorable event was the first concert of the company in December 1967.... An orchestra, three substantial works by three choreographers, [Peter Randazzo, Cynthia Barrett, and Patricia Beatty], sets and lights of a high calibre, funding by the Ontario Arts Council, visitors from New York City, eleven hundred curious audience members made it all a big event.

The New Dance Group not only set a type of precedent for the working relationship between the future founders of Toronto Dance Theatre, but also provided the financial stability on which the new company would later be based.

That first twelve concerts for The New Dance Group took place at the Ryerson Polytechnical Institute theatre. David Earle would be dancing with the company and Trish invited Peter Randazzo to choreograph and dance in a piece for the concert. She knew his work as a dancer with The Martha Graham Dance Company but was only formally introduced to him when he came to Toronto. Randazzo was staying with David Earle, now an intimate friend and professional colleague, and teaching a master class in Graham technique for Lilian Jarvis at the National Ballet School. Both Trish and Peter had tremendous energy and dynamic temperaments — and very different visions for the Ryerson concert. It is not surprising, given that this project was Trish's idea and built on her company, that the collaboration with Peter was not without its difficulties. She says, "I was making all the decisions. I was in all the pieces. I knew which ones needed more rehearsal and perhaps that's hard for others [to take]." Peter had difficulty in articulating his vision and was frustrated by Trish's passionate and forceful manner. Randazzo returned to New York, swearing never

to work with Patricia Beatty again! Beatty was unaware of this: "When the curtain rose on three of us at the Ryerson concert ... it was a sign." The concert was a success and this was due, in great part, to the mediation skills of David Earle. The pattern was set.

David Earle

1939 was the beginning of the "phoney" war in England but the volatile relationships in the Earle household in Toronto's west end were all too real to the second son, born September 17, just after the declaration of war. It was, for young David, like growing up in a theatre of war with the battle line drawn between himself and his brother. As his father had done for him, Mr. Earle groomed Douglas, his athletic eldest son to inherit the paternal family business, H.A. Kidd and Company, the largest button import company in Canada. David, the sensitive dreamy child, was drawn into his mother's camp. He remembers sitting on the stairs with Douglas, listening to his parents' incessant fighting. It is clear to him now that his parents were two unhappy souls caught in the mold expected of marriages in the Toronto society of the forties. In an article by Michael Crabb for *VanDance International*, Earle remembers, "I attempted to be a

peacemaker between my warring parents. The sound of my parents' anger was so hurtful. Even now anger is a sound I'll do anything to avoid." The role of arbiter was one that Earle was to play many times in the future.

David's parents did not share the same religious background (his father was an Anglican, his mother, a Christian Scientist); they compromised their spiritual beliefs by attending regular service at the "pseudo-gothic" Humbercrest United Church. Like many children, David's attention wandered during the long service, and he was attracted to the shapes of the church itself and its stain glass windows. This early introduction to ecclesiastical architecture and space inspired him. It was to be both a home and continuing theme for his dance making. "I think it is the stone, the glass, the music, and the poetry [that uplifts people] rather than the service." The Earle family attended Sunday church faithfully except when they all went to Peterborough to visit the paternal family farm where David's beloved grandmother lived.

David credits his grandmother with providing a sense of happiness, love, and assurance in his early life.

> Everything that is good in me is due to my grandmother.... My grandmother adored me. I could do anything, much to the annoyance of my parents. They would sit glaring at me.... Visits to Peterborough were heaven. It was freedom hall. I would dance and perform for my grandmother and fall at her feet, asking, "Was I good?" and she would reply, "You were very good."

His grandmother had a guest house with a library, and throughout his youth, holidays and summers were spent in this haven — his own magical kingdom.

David's mother, who had hoped that her second baby would be a daughter, encouraged David's artistic and creative nature. His experience in theatre began at the age of five when his mother sent him to ballet classes taught by the Birdsall sisters. Helen and Fanny Birdsall had opened their school in 1923 and over the course of the next sixty years, taught over nine thousand children. They believed their primary purpose was to enrich the lives of their pupils by instilling in them a love of dance and a strong sense of self-worth. Young David responded. It was not long before he was marrying his delight in dance with his father's business. "My first ballets were button ballets. I used to wander down the aisles of the button factory, filling my pockets with buttons.... I would use them to create dance formations ... there were corps buttons, solo buttons, duet buttons." Aunt Louise, who visited often to provide company for David's mother who insisted she could not live in a house "dominated by men," furnished the occasions for the creation of a season. David ("I was Diaghilev") created "thousands" of productions in the furnace room for Aunt Louise's pleasure, and she sat, generous with both her time and attention, in a straight-backed chair watching hours of David Earle original works.

From the age of eight, and for the next eleven years, David was a member of the Toronto Children's Players (TCP), a dramatic group run by Dorothy Goulding, youngest daughter of Denton Massey. In the winter, the children performed at Eaton Auditorium in a series of plays chosen and directed by Mrs. Goulding for young audiences. David remembers:

> Mrs. Goulding was a ferocious woman. When she staged a work she was the director par excellence with absolute control over the result. She held the script and gave you your line. She would have us say the line until we could produce the exact inflection she was looking for, and then it was yours to hold on to; we were all in terror of her.

The summers provided a magical reprieve. Mrs. Goulding enlisted the help of Barbara "Babs" McKay (who accompanied classes for the National Ballet of Canada) to play selected pieces of music on the piano for creative movement sessions. Other helpers, experienced professionals like Jack Medhurst and Charles Winter, assisted and guided the children to explore creative movement, drama, art, and music. The group would meet at Dentonia Park, the Massey estate, where Mrs. Goulding would have different areas of the grounds set up to accommodate the various disciplines of theatre: costumes, make-up, music, and movement. The children were divided into small groups to make up their own plays and then would move from area to area to dress their productions. By the end of the day they would have a performance created from the day-long experiential process. "Make-up was a great inspiration. I wanted to be beautiful and 'other.' Jack Medhurst would pair a younger child with an older child for make-up lessons. The older person would do half your face and you would have to do the other half to match. It was a great experience." David cites his years with the TCP as training from which he never recovered. "Imagine four times a year being in productions in beautiful costumes and make-up and lighting" which Mrs. Goulding "made happen" and then the lovely freedom of the summers' improvisations when Mrs. Goulding rarely interfered with their play making.

Business often took Mr. Earle to New York and he would bring back programmes from the shows he had seen on Broadway. David pored over the playbills. "I found tremendous Eros in the somewhat naked people — I thought they were gods and goddesses. I loved the glamour and beauty; it was almost religious." His visual and fantasy life was further inspired by the advertisements and columns in the Toronto papers and the performances to which he was taken. "I read about *Dark Elegies* and *Lilac Garden* and saw Lois Smith, David Adams, Lilian Jarvis, and Angela Leigh in these dramatic roles." He identified with romantic pieces about abandonment and rejection and with those tragic heroines whose lives were destroyed by the society in which they lived. He thinks that this rapport with the melancholy "other" may have been "partly growing up gay and under the protection of my older brother; perhaps because of my mother." Paradoxically, it was the creative opportunities in dance and theatre to explore the dark "other" in the safe environment of a metaphoric world which gave him the sense of completeness, happiness, and security which he had only experienced with his grandmother.

"An image addict," David enrolled in Radio and Television Arts at Ryerson Polytechnical Institute. He studied there for two years before accepting a scholarship to study ballet at the newly formed National Ballet School of Canada. At the age of twenty, he was a late entry into the school. He explains, "I was a special student at the ... school. Probably because they had no boys so they were willing to take even old ones to ... fill out the ranks for the large ballets." He goes on to add that he "had no idea what my potential was perceived to be" but that as "it wasn't the kind of place where you had a mature relationship with the staff," that sort of communication wasn't to be expected.

David trained for four years at the National Ballet School, during which time he met Donald Himes who was teaching Dalcroze Eurythmics there. Earle remembers being entranced by the music that Himes would improvise; it was, he says, "unbelievably refreshing" and different from the music played in ballet class. Himes himself had been taking modern dance training at the "Y" under the direction of Yoné Kvietys. Himes took Earle to the "Y" class and he was invited to join the performing troupe: "they also needed men." It was with this group that Earle did his first choreography and here that he met Susan Macpherson. They have remained friends and professional colleagues ever since.

The summer of 1963 was to change the direction of David's life. He went to Connecticut College to study with Martha Graham, José Limón, and Donald McKayle. Just as Beatty had felt released through modern dance, so David was captured by the nature of this new kind of movement. He remembers how the first time he saw the exercise, "turns around the back," he discovered it ended with a question: "It didn't go 'Ta Dum' as in ballet, it arrested my point of wonder." It was José Limón's teaching that was to inform David's entire life as a teacher: "He said 'of course we cannot teach you to dance in six weeks, but perhaps we can give you back something of yourself.' "

Danny Grossman, also a student that summer, offered David a place to stay in New York and that September, Earle moved to New York on a scholarship to train full-time at The Martha Graham School of Contemporary Dance. He lived at Danny Grossman's sixth floor walk-up for a time before moving out to share an apartment with James Cunningham, a childhood friend and fellow member of the Toronto Children's Players. Also studying at the Graham school were Donald Himes, Susan Macpherson, and Lilian Jarvis. Cunningham pointed out the other Canadian at the School. It was then that David, looking at Trish, said, "She's not Canadian." She was "pretty aggressive and too visible to be a Canadian."

One day in class, while sitting on the

floor, executing a diagonal high lift with both arms opening, David felt a sudden and unexpected strong pull on his back arm. He turned and found himself looking at the class demonstrator, Peter Randazzo. After class, he introduced himself and asked Peter if he wanted to go out for coffee and "that's how we met."

In 1966, Earle applied for and received his green card which made him eligible to work in the United States. He was unaware of another responsibility attached to holding a green card and which would soon alter the course of his career. Peter Randazzo was dancing in the off-season for the José Limón Company which was set to perform at the American Dance Festival at Connecticut College before proceeding on an American tour. Earle auditioned and was invited to join the company. He was already performing in the festival when he received a different sort of invitation from the government of the United States. "I went to lawyers and basically they told me [as a green card holder] they can draft any man of eligible age on American soil." Not wishing to go to Vietnam, Earle accepted the opportunity of a job in England from arts philanthropist Robin Howard.

Howard, an Englishman and a staunch supporter of Martha Graham and her company, financed Graham's second tour to England in 1963. Howard also provided funds for the training of British students in New York in the hope that they would bring their expertise back to England. Earle, as a citizen of a Commonwealth country, proved eligible for funding. He was invited to act as dance master and to dance with the group of Commonwealth dancers that Howard was assembling for the opening of Christ the King Cathedral in Liverpool. The idea of a sacred dance event appealed to David's sensibilities.

The cathedral was remarkable because, unlike the usual Anglican gothic architecture, the building was round. The congregation would worship in a circle with the altar at the centre. Peter likens it to a "space port." When the local ladies were asked to comment, they only remarked, "It will be luvely when it gets a bit of ivy on it!" The working conditions were miserable.

> Living conditions in Liverpool were so bad. We were staying in a hotel with no glass in the windows. It was cold and we had to keep getting up to put money in the meter to heat the room. We rehearsed in an unheated army barracks. The big forced air

heaters they brought in only warmed you if you were within six feet! I remember Susan Macpherson knitting. Wherever she went in rehearsal, it followed her. This thing just got longer and longer ... she was knitting her grief.

The company was horrified at the juxtaposition of such an extravagant building with the poverty that surrounded it and the sixty dancers finished the engagement wondering if the money might have been put to better uses.

In 1967, Earle moved to London to work with the newly formed London Contemporary Dance Theatre (LCDT), another company which benefited from Howard's sponsorship. Earle taught, danced, and toured with the company as well as assisting the artistic director, Robert Cohan. It was in December of the same year that Earle, who had come to know Trish Beatty at the Graham School and in guest appearances with her company in Toronto, returned home to appear in the New Dance Group of Canada's Ryerson concert.

Robert Cohan was in New York dancing with the Martha Graham Dance Company and so David returned to England for the winter of 1968 in order to direct the first season of the London Contemporary Dance Theatre, and then take them on a tour of England and Ireland. Earle was working on a season of original works with the LCDT at the University of London when he was visited by Peter Randazzo.

Peter Randazzo

Peter Randazzo was the youngest child born to a second generation Italian family in Brooklyn, New York, in 1943. He said he never felt as if he belonged. He was a frightened child, "totally insecure and totally fearful." His family did not seem to be interested in his ideas and he would sit and listen but never say much, thinking there was a whole world outside his family and that he would find it. At home, he was timid but out on the streets, he and his older brother were wild. He felt he was owned by his mother, and he disliked the Italian values and concepts of family life "where it becomes very tribal and you keep everything in.... I believe in freedom of the spirit and the individual ... in my family, I felt I was totally suppressed."

Until late in 1958, Randazzo had no interest in dance at all. He started dancing by accident. His girlfriend wanted to study modern dance at the Martha Graham School, but it was in Manhattan and she was afraid to go by herself. She begged Peter to take her. He remembers thinking that this kind of movement was "totally ridiculous" and could not understand why anyone would want to move that way. Then he saw Robert Powell, a dancer with the Graham company, who had a similar physique to his own. "He could do all this amazing stuff, and I couldn't do it at all.... I looked at his body and I looked at my body and said, 'If he can do it, why can't I?' So somewhere in my mind I thought I'll just stay here long enough to dance the way this guy is doing it." Randazzo's girlfriend dragged him to a scholarship audition. To her dismay, he received the scholarship and found himself "possessed with this insatiable appetite to do these things ..."

> I would literally tear my body apart whenever a teacher corrected me. In fact they stopped correcting me because they knew I was just insane. I would do anything they told me, to do the exercises the way they wanted. I was on fire to move. The result was that in two years, when I was seventeen and a half, I was on Broadway with the Martha Graham Dance Company.

When he was invited to join the company as a chorus member, he did not realize that this was a great honour, and he had to be coaxed to accept the offer.

Between 1961 and 1967, he toured with the company throughout the United States and Europe and fell in love with the founder. "I wasn't particularly interested in doing [Graham's] work, but I just became totally fascinated by her. I wanted to be around her as much as possible. She was very, very powerful and when she spoke, she seemed to have the accumulated knowledge of a thousand years. I thought, 'If I stay in the company, I'll be around her.'"

As a chorus member, Randazzo was at the lowest level in the company hierarchy. It was here that he learned to speak out and defend his viewpoint. He recalls that, "Every time I opened my mouth, somebody would slam me to the ground. I learned very well to sharpen my tongue to the point where no one dared speak to me because I could verbally bury them." Even though Randazzo was a chorus dancer, Graham treated him as if he were "King of the Hill." In return, he treated her like one of his friends in Brooklyn, calling her "Toots." This irreverence amused Graham; no one had ever dared deal with her like this before and, according to Randazzo, he and Martha had a "great time playing games with the company."

In his six years with the Martha Graham Dance Company, Miss Graham created nine parts for him. His employment with the company gave him $10.00 per week for two weeks' rehearsal and slightly more for the two weeks of Broadway performances. It wasn't enough to live on, however frugally, and it freed Randazzo to work with other choreographers and teachers and to make two American tours with the José Limón Dance Company.

But it was Graham who most deeply affected Randazzo as an individual and as an artist. She was larger than life. He absorbed her serious respect for dance. Accompanying his growing belief in himself as an artist ("I am a channel, a vessel through which energy flows"), was a driving intensity of purpose. He wanted to show what he believed to be the truth of his being in his work. "Graham's greatest gift was to show you 'you' ... but it was also a curse ... I said to myself, 'But I'm nineteen years old, what am I going to do with this? I can't be a totally evolved human being at nineteen....'" He began to use alcohol and drugs, although he never drank before a show, believing deeply in the power of the theatre as a stimulant. At nineteen, the passionate, obsessively driven Randazzo suffered a nervous breakdown and was hospitalized. Later that year, after therapy, he returned to the company and Graham warned everyone to leave "this boy" alone or they would be "out [of her company]."

For dancers in the 1960s, money was not a large consideration; their needs were pretty minimal: "My rent was $71 a month and you could live very well on five bucks for the weekend." When not dancing or studying or working in other companies, Randazzo supplemented his income with unemployment insurance and by coaching classes at the Graham School. It was through these classes that he met and became friends with David Earle. Lilian and David's invitation to come to Toronto in 1967, led to the meeting with Trish Beatty and her suggestion that Peter make a dance for the December performance at the Ryerson Theatre.

In this, his first foray into choreography, Peter created *Fragments* for himself, David, and Trish. While the concert was a success, the chemistry between Trish and Peter was stormy. He explains:

> The reason we didn't get along, I think, is basically where we were coming from. The difference of experience and lifestyle was in conflict. At the time, I was a very fast, angry person. I was just interested in getting things done in a hurry. My feeling in terms of the concert was there was a different perception going on in terms of the treatment of who had seniority, or priority. Whether it was my ego ... it could have been a million things, it could have been any one thing....

On his return to New York, Peter, still "fast and angry" and trigger-quick to react to anyone whom he perceived to be misusing "seniority," stood up to Martha Graham. The circumstances, as he describes them:

> We had a Clytemnestra rehearsal, and whenever there was a Clytemnestra rehearsal you knew it was [really a company] meeting because that was the only piece that had everybody in the company in it....
> I knew her body so well that when she walked in a room, I could tell you how she was going to behave. The worst sign [for] knowing that the wrath of God was coming was when she walked in the room with her back perfectly straight, her neck perfectly on her spine, her head about three inches above that, and she would walk very fast to the front....
> She walked into the room [moving] quickly to the front, turned, and with her right hand up, started into this rage. This was an even greater rage than I'd ever seen before so I started walking out of the room with my little dance bag and she started screaming at me. "Where are you going?" I said to her, "I'm leaving and if you want to talk to me you can phone me up." She went even wilder. I mean I had never seen this kind of anger from anything or anybody. I said, "If you want to talk

to me, you phone me up." Well, she was hop-
ping mad at this point and then she said, "I'll
slap your face," and she took a step towards
me. I said, "No, you won't." And I took a step
towards her. She looked in my eyes and I
looked in her eyes and she knew in that
instant that if she touched me I would have
killed her. There is no doubt in my mind that
I would have done that, I literally would have
ripped her head off. I said "If you want to talk
to me, you phone me up." Then I picked up
my little dance bag and walked out of the
room.

I didn't find out for a very long time after,
but no one moved for ten minutes. The room
was completely still for ten minutes, [then] ...
she walked out of the room. And that was my
leaving Martha Graham.

This confrontation left him angry, dejected, and unem
ployed. He made a spur-of-the-moment decision to visit
David Earle in London where David was working on the
season for the London Contemporary Dance Theatre.
While there, the two decided to collaborate and present a
concert of their own in Toronto.

On March 18, 1968, Peter Randazzo and David Earle
presented *Dance Concert* at the Toronto Workshop Productions Theatre, using Beatty's studio space for rehears-
als. *Dance Concert* was produced for them by Joan Fee,
then company manager for Trish. *Fragments* was once
again on the program but this time the female part
was danced by guest artist Noemi Lapzeson, a Graham alumna and a founding dancer with the London

Contemporary Dance Theatre. After the concert, Trish came backstage and said to Peter, "Well, you certainly are the dancer" and to David, "You certainly are the choreographer." Donald Himes explained, "Trish was ... the great, stunning lady of dance around [Toronto]. She had this wonderful body that did everything ... [she] was wonderful and inspiring but she could be seen as condescending." These two sensitive artists have yet to figure out exactly what she meant although she had been very supportive and generous from the beginning. After *Concert*, Earle returned to England to complete his commitments to Howard, but by the summer, both he and Randazzo returned to Toronto for good. For Randazzo especially, it was a kind of homecoming. He felt "like I belong here."

Before the two dancers returned for *Dance Concert*, they had had a conversation which had its own implications. One cold and rainy night in Liverpool, David and Peter were on a bus. Peter turned to David and said, "Let's start a dance company." David said, "What should we call it?" Peter said, "Toronto Dance Theatre." As easy as that. It was the start of a lifetime partnership together.

2

The Formation of the Toronto Dance Theatre

The experiences of presenting their own work suggested to Peter and David that the possibility of starting their own company was real. Discussions became concrete actions and before long they were negotiating with John Sime, founder and principal of the Three Schools of Art, to start their own company under his umbrella. Before they had signed the contract with Sime, Trish Beatty called them, offering her school and company as the base for their new venture. She was aware that Toronto could not support two companies and felt that joining forces would be the obvious solution. As well, as the sole choreographer for her company, she could not create new work fast enough to sustain a season and, "I was teaching so much and I was fund-raising.... I was keeping 22 Cumberland alive ... touring the universities.... I didn't realize what it required." This act of offering her solvent company and a thriving school to Earle and Randazzo exemplified Beatty's deep convictions about the importance of bringing the Martha Graham technique to Canada. She was never personally ambitious; she knew the task of pioneering for modern dance in Canada was greater than any one teacher, dancer, or director could undertake. Life experience taught her the

"A beautiful time of tremendous growth."

Peggy Baker, 1998

23

value of community, cooperation, and collaboration. Whatever happened, she just wanted to belong to it.

Peter and David were, naturally, somewhat wary of this gesture but after discussion, decided that it would be "gracious to accept the offer," with her participation. The three agreed that the new company would be called Toronto Dance Theatre. They apologized to John Sime for backing out of their deal but since Sime had already advertised classes, David taught at Three Schools of Art for the following year. Kenny Pearl (who was later to dance with Martha Graham and Alvin Ailey), "was my only regular student. I taught him private classes for a year to honour the contract, which was great because he became this famous dancer." Not only was this act in keeping with David's sense of honour, it was rewarding in that Pearl was such a delight to teach. It established

TOROnTO DAnce THEATre

Repertoire 1968

PRIMORDIAL (New Work)
Music: Andre Prevost
Choreography: Grant Strate
Design: John Bogaerts

TRAPEZOID (New Work)
Music: Donald Himes
        Ann Southam
Choreography: Peter Randazzo

MIRRORS (New Work)
Music: J. S. Bach
Choreography: David Earle

MOMENTUM
Music: Ann Southam
Choreography: Patricia Beatty
Set: Ursula Hanes

THE RECITATION
Music: Ann Southam
Choreography: David Earle

ANGELIC VISITATION #1
Music: Frank Martin
Choreography: David Earle
Set: Norberto Chiesa

ANGELIC VISITATION #2
Music: Ned Rorem
Choreography: David Earle

FRAGMENTS
Music: Eugene Lester
Choreography: Peter Randazzo

FLIGHT FANTASY
Music: Musitronic Productions
        Karol Rattray
        Georgi Nachoff
Choreography: Patricia Beatty
Set: Ursula Hanes

AFTERMATH
Music: Frank Martin
Choreography: Peter Randazzo

a relationship that would have an impact in the future of Toronto Dance Theatre.

The continued operation of what had been Beatty's school was an important element in the choreographers' plans. Through their teaching, they could hone their choreographic skills as well as train future dancers. The school also provided much needed revenue by offering thirty classes a week in modern dance technique, instruction in Dalcroze Eurythmics (taught by Donald Himes) and creative dance for children. No one had yet tried to start a modern dance company in Toronto that attempted to employ dancers full-time and, just as Lilian Jarvis had found other teaching for Trish, so teaching in the school provided additional income for the dancers. Susan Macpherson recalls the enthusiasm: "They called me and said would I like to come back [from New York] and dance with the Toronto Dance Theatre? They were making a company, and they would pay me a salary, and I could teach in their school, and I could make their costumes, and I could dance with the company, and I said, 'Yes!' " Despite personality clashes, drive and determination were the strength of the founders' union and their pioneering spirits infected their company and "they were heady and exciting times."

In December 1968, on the three Monday evenings before Christmas, eight pieces, performed by nine dancers at Toronto Workshop Productions Theatre, marked the beginning of what is now Toronto's oldest professional modern dance company.

Making It All a Bit More "Legitimate"

In the late sixties and early seventies, "Toronto the Good" was a relatively uncorrupted, quiet, and conservative small city. It was a place of parks; people left their doors unlocked and their keys in their cars; newspaper boxes had no glass and it seemed as if there was church on every corner. Toronto was infamous for its "blue laws" and its Sunday closings. It was, says Peter, "very cute and clean with friendly and open people. I thought I was in Thornton Wilder's *Our Town*. It was incredible ... the first time.... I arrived on Washington Avenue [Donald Himes' home] I felt this sense of calm come over me that I had never experienced before in my life."

His arrival, however, coincided with less "quiet" times. The shift from financial and social position as determinants of "who you were" to a more accepting attitude, allied to free expression, exploration of the body, examination of the psyche, Eastern philosophies, and experimentation with mood-enhancing drugs, left some citizens floundering and defensive. For the young and the more "forward-thinking" Torontonians, however, Toronto Dance Theatre, created by three passionate and zealous artists who believed intensely in the profundity of their art form, embodied the sense of change. "It was," recalls Peggy Baker, "a beautiful time of tremendous growth."

By April 1969, the founders had established the mandate of Toronto Dance Theatre. This document confirms in very clear and concise terms, the commitment of the three founders to the school and to performance as the primary vehicles for educating the public both locally and nationally. It established TDT as a non-profit corporation, with Randazzo, Beatty, and Earle as the first directors.

The choice of who held what position was arbitrary: Peter became president since he "liked" the Presidential Seal he had seen in the lawyer's office, David was to be vice-president and Trish (in accordance with the "mores" of the time: "I was the girl") became secretary-treasurer. An advisory board was appointed from members of the community who supported their efforts and was in place by May of 1969. Douglas Earle and Clifford Beatty remained with the board for the next twenty-five years. The brothers were always available to supply business advice and to provide emotional support. They were, says Trish, "the foundation of the organization ... our older brothers who listened and helped out with everything." Two other members of this first advisory board, Anglican minister, Clifford Elliott, and Catholic priest, Peter Sheehan, were sympathetic to the founders' sense of spirituality. David explains:

> They made us feel that the community had an appetite for us. They provided openings to non-conventional audiences where people's expectations were more in line with what we wished to communicate.... They really cared, they felt that something had come into the community that was going to add to their ministry.

Although their ideals were now set down in writing, the founders did not make long-term plans for their achievement. "I think we wanted to produce a company that would ... give a lot of Toronto seasons and do our work all the time. It was pretty immediate. I don't think we presumed it would go on forever, just to the next event," said David. The company was to be a vehicle for the founders' choreographic endeavours. Touring and reputation would naturally grow from this. Tangible long-term goals ranked second to the experience of creating the work.

Creating the Work: One

The founders were committed to bringing the powerful and visceral Graham technique, embedded with the sensibilities of the ritual act, to Canadian audiences. They were not, in Peggy Baker's words, "trying to be her." David always claimed they were dancing in Graham's "light": "I'm not interested in something *new* — I'm interested in what is *true*." For all three, the Graham technique was a doorway through which they passed to explore their own truths.

Nine months after the company formed, writer Herbert Whittaker asked the founders, "What has brought the Toronto Dance Theatre to such notice in a field generally thought barren for anyone but ballet dancers?" David Earle suggested that one strength was their choreography: "We all differ in choreography. The opportunity to explain new movement is all we ask. Peter is closest to it. He's instinctive.... Trish says she will always be a 'head' dancer [Beatty qualifies Earle's term to mean she is a conscious dancer].... I am very concerned with love generally and oriented to the past."

Of the eight works created by David between 1967 and 1969, four explored themes of the Christian tradition: *Angelic Visitation #1* and *#2*, *Fire in the Eye of God*, and *A Thread of Sand*, a narrative of the memories of Mary Magdalene which drew on David's knowledge of Medieval and Renaissance art (and which was referred to by the newspapers as a fifty minute opus on the sex life of Jesus Christ). About *Lovers*, created in 1969, Ralph Hicklin wrote:

Lovers ... is more complex. With four couples, [Earle] explores the establishment of relations between — and among — four men and four women. The relations vary from love to hate, in varying levels of intensity. When I say they are reminiscent of ballets such as *Lilac Garden*, *Age of Anxiety*, and *Jeux* [which were all part of the classical ballet's repertoire at the time], I don't suggest that there is lack of originality. Rather I mean that Earle has been evocative in the best possible way.

Peter's choreographic outpourings explored pure movement as an abstract mathematical or geometric construct representing, in its strong, physical undertones, the conflict between power and social status, and the darker relationships between men and women. In 1968, he collaborated with Ann Southam, the composer, and Donald Himes to create *Trapezoid*, an abstract piece with an electronic score. In 1969, he again collaborated with Southam to create *Encounter*, which explores power as the destructive element in a male/female relationship. This time it was Peter's turn to have *Lilac Garden* used as a reference point. Nathan Cohen, in *The Toronto Star*, remarked on the "eloquent simplicity" and the "interesting similarities" to Antony Tudor's work. Peter did examine narratives, building on the Cain and Able story told from Cain's perspective, for *I Had Two Sons*. *Continuum*, first presented in the repertoire in 1969, revealed how his use of the Graham vocabulary had evolved. Lawrence O'Toole, writing in 1976, describes *Continuum* as "pure sustained

movement without a thought of any emotion behind it....
A continuous line of movement — that is all it is ... and
it can hold you spellbound."

From the beginning, Trish's work was an expression
of her emerging life philosophy. It was cleanly struc-
tured, intense and sensual, highly dramatic and theatrical. *Momentum*, first created in the New Dance Group
and reworked in 1969, is based on the relationship of
Macbeth and Lady Macbeth (Ann Southam nicknamed
Trish, "Lady MacBeatty"). Trish created two solos, *Flight
Fantasy* and *First Music* (most recently performed in 1998
by Grace Miyagawa) that probed the depths of her own
psyche. Perhaps the most dramatic of these early works

was *Against Sleep*.
Beatty cites this
work as "probably
my first conscious
spiritual statement."
This exploration of
the temptation of
suicide became a
signature work in
which Trish and
David danced to-
gether. This time,
the critic's compari-
son was perhaps
more relevant. Ralph
Hicklin wrote:

> Miss Beatty [has] established a new stature
> for herself.... At times, she evoked a young
> Martha Graham, so positive was she ... Her
> mastery ... and Earle's, both physically and
> in conception, pushed the evening into enor-
> mous suspense and equal satisfaction.

The first works of the founders reflect their individual experiences and early inspirations and were to be
mined and explored over their lifetimes. With each piece,
the creators evolved; stronger works stayed in the repertoire, others were dropped to make way for new composi-
tions. Susan Macpherson remembers the long hours of
hard work, the family feeling and the kind of energy that
was driving everyone. She credits this extraordinary sense
of generation: "Because all three choreographers were so

different, the vitality of the company was kept alive."
After the two years of operation, there were eighteen
works in the repertoire, representing a diversity of styles,
with great appeal for their heterogeneous audiences. In
1970, growing success demanded relocation and TDT
moved into new quarters at 26 Lombard Street.

Inky Fingers

The founders' vision of art for art's sake began its
long engagement with reality: the economic necessities of
running a company. The three ran the business as best
they could. When one person was teaching, another would
be rehearsing or choreographing and the third would be
on the telephone trying to arrange a booking. David
explained the method of planning and decision making
was to Barbara Gail Rowes:

> The company really runs on a democratic
> ethic. Everybody can develop in whatever role
> is suitable to his abilities in terms of his ego
> ... we just take sides and begin to argue the
> issue until it's resolved to everybody's satis-
> faction. Sometimes it takes days. But we find
> it the resolution of our needs at the moment.

Rowes goes on to describe Toronto Dance Theatre as "an artistic commune in which individual spirits can live in harmony while developing their creative energies with fanatic dedication." Peggy Baker remembers that the company was "like a little hippy tribe ... they all had relationships with each other ... it was all very interwoven." Beatty who was wearing "funky" clothes long before Toronto was assaulted with tie-dye and purple, sees it from another perspective: "We were very 'in' with the hippies we knew. Here we were, teaching this serious modern dance. They thought this was 'it' ... I was terribly thrilled that they thought I was a swinger, too. The dope that we all took at parties was to celebrate, not to escape." Her own wedding in 1971 to young dancer Clifford Martin Duck brought together the highly unlikely worlds of dance, "hippydom," and the upper middle class of "old Toronto." "It was a smash. David in his white caftan, and Peter in his hip Brooklyn suit, said they looked more like the bride and groom than we did dressed in our cream colours."

Harmony was tested in the matter of finances; all of them were involved. "Peter is very good with facts and figures," says Earle, and "all we did was divide what we had between the number of people we had." Macpherson confirms this practice: "I taught classes, made costumes, rehearsed, designed, and performed for $40 a week. That was really big money in those days, except a lot of the time there wasn't $40 so we split whatever was in the bank account."

What was in the bank account was, in the beginning, financial backing from the Beatty family. "We couldn't have started if we hadn't personally known people who have money, and who don't care whether we're good enough," Beatty explained to Herbert Whittaker. The Ontario Arts Council gave them $1250 the first year ("That's really trust!"), and in the second year, it raised the grant to $2500. Then the Canada Council "phoned us to ask what we were doing for money. They told us they would be happy to receive our application ... and they supported us right away" with a grant of $2000.

Although exciting and challenging at first, the process of applying to government agencies for funding did not come easily to the founders. Once they realized they could get grants, they spent considerable time filling out forms. "We always had ink on our hands while working in the studio," Earle continues: "I remember we were all working to fill out this grant application to the Ontario

Arts Council. We all took turns typing it because none of us could type. One of us would blow it and then the next person would take over, this went on all night!"

The primary fund-raiser for the company was Trish Beatty. She would arrange fund-raising parties to which the founders would go to meet Beatty family connections and collect donations. Clifford Beatty explains: "Father supported Toronto Dance Theatre, not in a major way directly. He had friends and associates who would help out. People like the Laidlaws were great friends. Father was helpful in getting bank loans as a guarantor. He was on the hook for ten years but the bank never called the guarantee." In fact, in those days the banks were willing to take the risks associated with funding the arts, and their trust is something that the founders remember with gratitude. One of the most generous patrons was Ann Southam, one of the company's resident composers and a long-time supporter of the company.

Although dancing regularly, Beatty's fund-raising and teaching commitments made it almost impossible to find the time to create her dances. She says, "I realized it was a full-time job. I could either spend time raising money or working in the studio. I wanted to be in the studio." David and Peter were also finding it difficult to both create and administer. They began to look for someone to assume the position of manager.

At the time, James Plaxton was working with the company. Like Susan Macpherson who was undertaking a multiplicity of roles, Plaxton designed sets, carried the portable dance floor, designed lights, drove the truck, stage managed and, when on tour, was the company manager. As Plaxton (a non-dancer) says, he "did everything but laundry and make costumes." By 1971, the founders believed they had found someone who understood their philosophy, could handle all the business aspects and not interfere artistically. As would often happen in the history of this company, they turned to one of their own and asked Plaxton if he "would like to come and be our guy" in an administrative capacity.

"Our Guy" in Charge

When Plaxton began his job in September 1971, he inherited the administration of a facility (which soon took over more space and changed its address to 34 Lombard Street), a school, a dance company, a budget that accounted for thirty-five performances, and the responsibility for finding the venues in which the company could perform. The touring circuit included churches, community centres, and universities across southern Ontario. They offered the kind of non-traditional places for performance that suited the educational and aesthetic goals of the founders. "Performances" included lecture demonstrations, teaching workshops, and excerpts of works in the repertoire, as well as performing the works in full.

The school offered two different levels of classes given in the morning and in the evening and, as there were now two studios, it meant that more than one class could be taught at a time. The style of teaching was steeped in the Graham philosophy and there was an element of mystery to the approach. Like the Graham studio in New York, there was a sense that it was taboo to take classes elsewhere or to train in any other mode, even though the founders themselves had a broad background of training. "[Others in the company] had lots of ballet but if you had a scholarship at TDT," recalls Peggy Baker, "you were not allowed to take ballet, even though part of how they [the founders] became the dancers they were was because of that training." Baker felt this lack in her own background so keenly that later on, she left a developing career to study ballet in New York.

At the time, however, Peggy was more than thrilled to be a part of the school. She remembers those early days:

> If you were a serious student, it meant taking class first thing in the morning, going off to your part-time job, then coming back in the late afternoon for another class. Company dancers would rehearse all day and teach the evening classes. A class card cost $50 and meant that you could take as many classes as you wanted in a month.

Students with potential and little money were given scholarships, as Baker was for her advanced training. Toronto Dance Theatre was known as "Freedom Hall" because they gave away so many classes. Trish explains "The reason we did that was not because we were bad administrators, but because we wanted to start an art form in this part of the world." The generosity was an important stepping stone in developing a well-grounded company.

Fund-raising was not one of Jim Plaxton's strengths. But by 1971, mainly due to Trish Beatty's efforts, the company was being funded by the Municipality of Metropolitan Toronto, the Atkinson Foundation, the E.W. Bickle Foundation, the Floyd S. Chalmers Foundation, and the Laidlaw Foundation, in addition to the Councils. As the financial picture became a little more secure and as company members were busy teaching, choreographing, and rehearsing, they could not be depended upon to help with administration and production. Plaxton began to hire a conventional staff. He continued to design sets and lighting but less frequently. Ron Snippe was hired to design lights, there was a new stage manager, and Plaxton searched for a new costume designer to relieve an overworked Susan Macpherson. Snippe remembers, "I didn't know much about dance, it was baptism under fire." Plaxton also began, with the founders enthusiastic support, to plan for a company tour to England. Touring, they all recognized, would extend the company's reputation and lengthen the season. It could also mean that, with good revues from abroad, the Canadian artists' maxim, "You have to go away to be recognized in Canada" would come into play, expanding the home audiences and enhancing revenues. Good reviews would also be helpful in supporting grant applications. Touring, however, does not come "cheap" as they all knew when they first explored the idea with the London Contemporary Dance Theatre in 1968.

"The Place" to Be

The National Ballet of Canada had a European tour planned for May–June of 1972. Since the tour would begin in London, Plaxton arranged to "piggyback" Toronto Dance Theatre's advertising on that of the National Ballet. The appearance of Toronto Dance Theatre at The Place Theatre in London in early May was to serve as a warm-up for the arrival of the National Ballet of Canada at the Sadler's Wells Theatre later that month.

Although TDT was subsidized by public funds, the trip to England was almost entirely self-financed. In

England, they went to a photo shoot with the internationally renowned dance photographer, Anthony Crickmay. The irony was that the pictures were so expensive they couldn't afford to purchase them all. Despite the company's poverty, this first international tour did well at the box office and the critics praised the production values. They did not, however, understand or like all the choreography. Craig Dodd's review in *The Dancing Times* is a good example of the response:

> Peter Randazzo, the most Grahamized (as in pasteurized or hypnotized) of the directors, was a clear winner in the obscurity stakes. He certainly has an eye for theatre and devised slick, theatrical packages. Unfortunately what they contain, if anything, is never revealed clearly enough to the audience.... Miss Beatty's other contributions were, I am afraid, second only to Mr. Randazzo's for obscurity ... audience response was enthusiastic. The theatre was packed every night

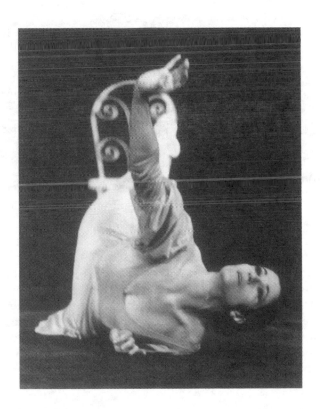

and the company, which is not in the habit of taking curtain calls, at least lurked behind long enough to hear the great applause.

The results, in spite of the Ontario Arts Council's warning not to go, were worth it and the Canadian Broadcasting Company (CBC) was impressed enough to document their first international tour. Two of the works were filmed "on location": *Dark of the Moon*, the legend of the witch boy choreographed by Peter, was filmed on a moonlit night at Stonehenge; Trish's *Rhapsody in the Late Afternoon*, in the garden of Westminister Abbey. (She remembers that it was freezing and kept warm by the sherry liberally supplied by the canon.) *Starscape* was filmed on stage and shows in overlapping versions with both Peter and David dancing the role. After London, the company performed in Paris, and then went on holiday. It had all been a great success.

Fame without Fortune

The audiences in the first years of TDT were made up of university intellectuals, visual artists, and, as Graham Jackson describes it, "the exotics — girls with high cheek bones and tropical flowers in their hair, men with capes and elaborate drawls." Many followers of the company treated them almost like movie star, "People were crazy about this company and they were crazy about individual people in the company. Barry Smith probably had hundreds of young women who were just insane over him and these people ... thronged to performances and would come night after night." Ralph Hicklin wrote in *The Telegram* in February 1969:

> Audiences in Toronto for modern dance programs reacted with the same near hysterical enthusiasm that used to characterize ballet audiences when the Russian idiom was still unusual, even shocking. It's the kind of enthusiasm that one commentator unkindly labelled "the lunatic fringe." And it is the kind of enthusiasm that last night greeted the first of three programs to be given by Toronto Dance Theatre ... the applause, the cheers that greeted each work on the program were of ovation proportions ... ovations were not out of place ... [TDT] has presented some of the most exciting theatre to be seen in Toronto.

Trish and Peter each had a following. Trish was stunning to watch with long thick dark hair, a languid, lithe figure and dancing which incorporated slow sustained movements, liquid leg extensions and her beautifully arched feet. She was also a model for her followers in dress, thought, and intensity. Peggy Baker remembers, "[She] wore Birkenstocks which I'd never seen ... and hipster bell bottom knit pants ... and she would say these really profound things and we would just be knocked out." For some, who preferred their charismatic women on film rather than in the flesh, she was merely "loud," but for many, Trish Beatty was a dramatic, self-assured and flamboyant figure both on and off the stage.

Peter also had a dynamic, intense quality. "He was like walking electricity with sparks flying off in every direction. He vibrated at such a level and generated so much energy for dance, he was almost scary to be around." He was adamant about what constituted dance, technique, and choreography and was prepared to go to war to defend his ideas. Donald Himes remembers the violent energy between Peter and Trish when they disagreed: "They would never listen to each other. David was always the big pacifier between these two forces. He was very protective of Pete and wanted to keep him sane and going." Peter and Trish rarely danced in each other's work; when they did appear together, it was usually in one of David's pieces. Despite all the attention they garnered, Trish and Peter did not get caught up in either their own popularity or arguments to the detriment of their art. Freed from administration, all three founders continued to evolve and create extraordinary theatre and dance.

Most of the concerts in the early seventies were held at Toronto Workshop Productions. Its small theatre limited the size of audiences but meant that TDT sold out every night. "People were crazed when they got there ... just going wild for every dance ... I was so shocked and exhilarated to see all these other people sharing my own passion about what was going on." Heady times, indeed; the world was in social upheaval, culture was being redefined and TDT and its three creative "genies" were out of the bottle and at the heart of the new expression in Toronto, the Not-so-Good anymore.

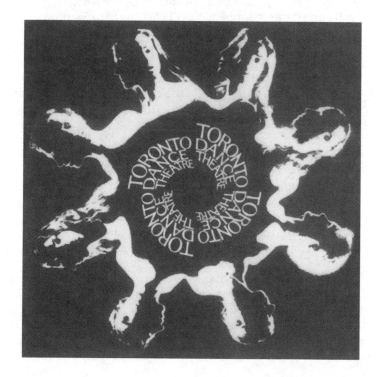

New Dances and Nudity

With more time available in the studios and somewhat less worry about administration, the founders were able to concentrate more fully on choreography. Peter's creation, *Dark of the Moon*, used Robert Daigneault's electronic score of eerie pops and dissonant squeaks to create a sense of foreboding. Barry Smith's speed, flexibility, and sinuous contractions were breathtaking to watch. *Starscape*, filmed by CBC with both Peter and David, was also performed by Smith, each dancer bringing his own unique qualities to the image of a star slowly blinking and weaving as it journeys across the night sky. In 1971, Peter made *Prospect Park*, a work inspired by sculptures in a park, and the ritualistic *Visions for a Theatre of Mind. Untitled Solo* made a great impression on at least one audience member. The piece is about the birthing process. "A dancer inside a cloth tube enacts a sculptured struggle that gives an unending flow of images ... until freed of the cloth, the dancer stands naked." When performed at Walter Court at the Art Gallery of Ontario, one of the security staff, seeing Amelia Itcush perform, invited a group of his buddies to see the show the next night. But the casting had changed. When Peter emerged from the tube, the man was heard to exclaim, "It was a chick last night, I swear it was a chick!"

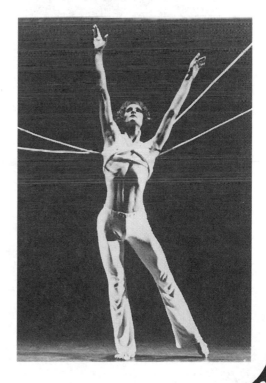

Nudity had naturally developed as something which offered itself to be explored. David was commissioned by the Guelph Spring Festival and, using the device of an operetta within an operetta, the result was a multi-media work exploring the archetypes of opera. Amusing to the younger generation, it was an effrontery to the older. But Herbert Whittaker enjoyed it all:

With the inevitability of fashion, nudity hit the ... Festival on Saturday night but it was so gentle, discreet, and pastoral that the audience could only be enchanted ... onto the screen their nude cinema images were projected in a sylvan setting. The audience widened its eyes, squinted, then laughed as the dancers went skittering into the spring foliage in a Keystone romp.

Operetta became one of David's few light choreographic works and it was especially popular on the university circuit where students admitted that the dance had "some pretty groovy hips."

David also explored nudity in a more serious manner. *Portrait*, created on Susan Macpherson, examines the fall from grace of the mistress of the King of France in the "age of magnificence." There is a poignant moment when the courtesan's maids take down the top of her gown, place her jewels upon her bare breast and hand her a mirror. The exquisite stillness with which Macpherson gazes at her reflection, conveys to us her knowledge that this favour will pass and she, too, will be retired into obscurity. Like the courtesan, *Portrait* was retired from the repertoire after a year.

David continued to explore deep mythological narratives. *Legend* is the tale of the rite of passage of an Indian boy to manhood. *The Silent Feast* examines the story of Salomé and John the Baptist. William Littler enthusiastically describes the work:

> And what a chorus! Its members wear rags, climb through and over walls, break into barbaric dances and generally behave in the manner of furies. The stage often explodes in movement as the chorus shoves around the modular elements of Jim Plaxton's set, now turning them into a wall to be broached, now a jury box, now a bier. The dancing itself incorporates a rich vocabulary of movements, some reminiscent of African Tribal dances, some redolent of the east, some as severely ritualistic, as others are abandoned.

Many of these elements were to be revisited in David's future work, *Court of Miracles*.

Trish, continued to fund-raise and teach (as did Peter and David) but compared to Peter and David her output was limited. She created *Rhapsody in the Late Afternoon*, a piece that "is a lyric fantasy with an element of surrealism — a rendezvous." It was only after her siblings saw the work that she realized she was dancing about her parents' relationship. In 1970, responding to social issues, Trish created *Hot and Cold Heros* (the title taken from a sign in a New York delicatessen) to the music of Jimi Hendrix, The Rolling Stones, and Ann Southam. The piece explored the "communion between those who 'swing' and those whose lives appear less glamourous."

Peter continued to be creatively prolific with *The Amber Garden*, *The Three-Sided Room*, and the vicious satire of *The Last Act*. David's important contribution (and still a favourite of his) was *Boat, River, Moon* — a tale told in the Japanese style which, David feels, is his "truly original" distillation of the saga of life, death, and resurrection. David's experiences with the Toronto Children's Players continued to inform his vision and his massive work of 1973 was *Atlantis*. It had fifteen dancers (apprentices and guests were used), was divided into five parts, and lasted half an hour. John Fraser from *The Globe and Mail* remarked that it:

has all the hallmarks of a classic creation; here the constituent parts, movements, music drama, sets, and costumes conspire to produce a completeness and unity that is depressingly rare in any of the arts.... *Atlantis* dazzles and inspires as it takes your breath away in its beauty both visually and conceptually.

The works in the repertoire were not all austere and weighted in philosophy, designed to make an audience think deeply. David delighted audiences again with the humour of *The Ray Charles Suite*. "It was," says Trish, "divine!" Using the metaphor of the high school dance, David used this context to explore "the relations that were going on in the company, who danced with whom and who picked whom. It was wonderful ... very vivid!"

Trish created a piece for David which capitalized on his Chaplinesque qualities. Entitled *Harold Morgan's Delicate Balance*, the work incorporates Trish's sense of humour. "A comical look at the erotic fantasies which occupy insurance salesman Harold Morgan's mind while travelling on a GO train," David was looked wonderful in his silk pyjamas. It was unfortunate that the dresser had put them in the dryer one night because they shrunk to his knees and he looked more "like a little boy" than the salesman. Laundry problems apart, the work was difficult to tour because "it had a set which no theatre in the country could hold."

Gloom and Doom and Taking a Bow

Although works were reviewed and praised, there was often a qualifying "but" from the reviewers. As early as 1969, Ralph Hicklin was asking, "Must everything be serious to the point of glumness?" In 1971, Barbara Gail Rowes commented, "It is obvious from just one performance of the Toronto Dance Theatre that their intensity and self-conscious individualism is no less serious or zealous than a religious movement." In 1973, Selma Odom remarked that "[the] shadow of Graham's approaches to psychological drama and of Horst's emphasis on formal

structure and style is frequently all too apparent." One of the most contentious issues with the press was the company's refusal to take bows. David explains their reasoning:

> There was a huge initial response. We actually did curtain calls at the beginning. That response was unreasonable considering we were just getting started. We hoped it was good work but it wasn't always great work. We began to suspect that we were being buoyed up by a kind of appetite engine that wasn't exactly connected to who we were and what we were doing. We were filling a void for some people who wished there was some energy in dance that was erotic, intense, and compelling, and other than the National Ballet. So it was our decision to make a more austere world for people to come to because we didn't want them to dismiss the philosophic content of our work.

Of this decision Trish comments, "We realized later it was well meaning, but too harsh." The refusal to take curtain calls often left their audiences "going out of their minds," according to Peggy Baker, but "they [the founders] were serious, serious artists." Trish and David broke with this established TDT protocol once in 1973 at Banff where she and David performed *Against Sleep* in lieu of a student performance. After tremendous applause, Trish turned to David and said, "We have to honour that." They did, but it was several years before they would resume taking bows.

The Toronto arts scene was growing and changing and audiences began to want more variety from Toronto Dance Theatre. They wanted lighter entertainment. They were, as Plaxton put it, "tired of sacred, classical, religious experiences." The reputation for serious work so earnestly fostered by the triumvirate and their dancers was, of course, not a true reflection of the repertoire which included a good number of "lighter" crowd pleasers. In particular, one has achieved the status of a legend.

Babar

When company members indicated that they, too, wanted to choreograph, the founders were surprised. However, they encouraged their dancers to choreograph and provided rehearsal time and performance opportunities, either as studio workshops or as presentations when the company was touring. They also invited collab-

oration from artists known to them. One such artist was their good friend, Donald Himes, who was now teaching at the school and had already created a work for the company, *Songs From The Newfoundland Outports* (1971). In Donald's final year of studying Dalcroze Eurythmics in Geneva in 1959, the students had done a performance of the de Brunhoff children's tale of the little elephant *Babar* to the music of Franz Poulenc. Donald had always wanted to do another production. In December 1971, in association with the Toronto Dance Theatre, Donald Himes presented *Babar*. This production, a real departure for the company, ran for a week during the Christmas holidays and was a huge success. Because of the expensive royalties for both the music and the story, and the outlay to make the costumes, the production did not bring in a lot of revenue. However, *Babar* soon proved to be a hit as children's theatre and a new market opened for the company — school touring. Performing *Babar* in schools became a part of the company's bread and butter outreach programming. Donald reflects on its popularity: "At one time when the name Toronto Dance Theatre was mentioned, people would say 'Oh, *Babar!*'" Not wanting to be known as a "children's theatre" company (always considered by adult professionals in any of the performing arts as a "kiss of death"), nevertheless *Babar* became the School of Toronto Dance Theatre's signature performing piece.

Susan Cash explains the importance of *Babar* for her:

When I was in the professional programme at Toronto Dance Theatre, I played baby Babar for two years. It was such an engaging tale narrated by its director and venerable leader, Donald Himes. The more seasoned company dancers would make fun of us having to do it but, in a way at that time, *Babar* was a "rite of passage" at TDT. *Babar* taught me a lot about theatre. We got to perform in very big, heavily unionized theatres to crowds of eager children and their parents. Some said at that time we were playing better theatres than the company.

What was most challenging and rewarding was wearing this huge painted and glued foam elephant costume and still getting the emotional sense across. Even though I was baby Babar I had to be larger than life under that costume. I lost two pounds a show because I had to work so hard and the costume was hot. The visibility was poor, and we were always bumping into other animals onstage. One time Tedd Robinson who was in *Babar* at that time, fell off the stage into the orchestra pit. Lucky for him he was an elephant too, therefore well padded. When I did baby Babar, Murray Darroch was the old man. I was always flinging myself at him onstage till one day, offstage, he gave me a severe reprimand for being out of control. It was true. When I put on that costume it was like I was entering another world, like that of a child. When I was sad and upset, I genuinely wept.

I learned much from every experience I had at Toronto Dance Theatre and playing baby Babar contributed to enriching my theatrical experience which has served me well in my independent dance life.

For sixteen years, *Babar* was a rite of passage for the dancers who went through the school.

Reality Strikes Again

The company's seasons in Toronto were mainly presented at Toronto Workshop Productions theatre or the MacMillan Theatre. In 1971, they felt ready for the much larger venue at St. Lawrence Centre. But, in spite of the extraordinary output and successes, by 1972 the company faced its first financial crisis and ceased operations for four months over the summer. John Fraser explained the situation in an article for *The Globe and Mail*:

The company's biggest problem, and this is directly tied to its financial plight, is that modern dance has been very hard to establish in Canada. Audiences have been growing but there were still many empty seats during its last Toronto season at St. Lawrence Centre. "We still owe the St. Lawrence $2,500," said Plaxton, "but as we get more established our financial problems seem to get more complex.... Our rent for our studios ... went up from $500 to $1,400 in one year and we really can't move because we've already

invested $12,000 here, so it's all a bit of a
bind. Still, we're determined to survive.

Whenever the company had this type of cash flow problem, Trish could fall back on the generosity of her family
to keep the company operational.

In 1973, to encourage audiences to experience modern
dance and to increase their income, the founders hosted
what they called an *"At Home"* series. They decorated
their studios and offered an event each week. Speakers
such as Walter Sorrell, noted dance scholar and critic
from New York, were featured. Lecture demonstrations
were given, and pieces of repertoire were shown. To promote discussion and an appreciation of dance, slides and
films of dance works were shown. It was a successful concept borrowed from their touring program and brought
people from the community into the company's personal
space; it was to be the first of many community activities
they would host. It did not, however, generate much additional revenue.

Financial strain continued to haunt the company and
Plaxton found himself in the office trying to juggle figures, coordinate schedules, promote seasons, and still be
creative with his set and lighting designs. Not surprisingly, he became disenchanted with administration. The
company needed an administrator who was also a fund-
raiser. Enter Roger Jones.

3 HISTORY DOES NOT develop in a straight line nor events in isolation, and the evolution of Toronto Dance Theatre did not occur in a vacuum. In 1970, York University initiated its dance program and by 1974, many of the graduating class were founders and dancers of a new company, Dancemakers. Peter, Trish, and David encouraged and supported these new members of the dance community by giving them free classes and studio space for two years. They gave generously knowing from their own experience how hard it was to start a company, and knowing the dancers would put their generosity to good use. They expected nothing in return.

That same generosity embraced other dancers looking for a chance to learn a different dance technique. By 1973, dancers from the National Ballet School and Company, such as Karen Bowes-Sewell, Karen Kain, Timothy Spain, Ann Ditchburn, and David Hatch Walker (a former student of Trish's) were "sneaking off" to take classes at TDT. "Miss O" (Betty Oliphant, principal of the school), in a familiar echo of the founders' way of thinking, did not approve of students taking classes elsewhere. But for some dancers, neither the National Ballet nor Toronto Dance Theatre supplied the freer experimental atmosphere that many were searching for.

" ... when do you ever feel secure? Or is it important?"

Peter Randazzo, 1978

Jennifer Fisher cites the inaugural concert on June 13, 1972, of what was to become 15 Dance Lab, as a "sort of post-ballet moment that kick-started Toronto into the post-modern era." Unofficially led by former National Ballet dancers Lawrence and Miriam Adams, the concert is best remembered for Miriam's *ode to yogurt* and Lawrence's physical violation of a brick wall to the soundscape of a Nixon speech on Vietnam. This concert filled a niche for the disenchanted and the avant-garde, and was the first example of a dance event happening in a non-institutional manner: a group of dancers coming together to explore what they wanted to explore and making it happen. They did not get paid; the experience was about finding their own way to make their dances happen. These concerts continued until, in 1974, 15 Dance Lab, a small performance space, was opened by Lawrence and Miriam Adams to support alternative development in dance.

In 1973, The Dance Office of the Canada Council convened a steering committee to assess the feasibility of a national organization in response to the growing dance activity across Canada. The result of the committee was the formation of The Dance in Canada Association. The intent of this non-profit association was to represent professional dance companies across the country and to encourage, promote, and establish communication in the dance field. It provided a forum for education and the stimulation of ideas through an annual conference, and it was to advise new companies and individuals on funding sources and administration issues. The association was also to publish *Dance in Canada* Magazine and a bilingual monthly newsletter. The inherent difficulty with the concept was the expectation on the part of everyone that the association would be all things to all people in the dance community. For such a disparate group of organizations and of people (the term "independent artist" had just come into use) it was an impossible dream but, for over a decade, it became a unifying source for dance across the country.

The Managing Director

It was into this burgeoning and chaotic period for dance, that Roger Jones stepped. He came to Toronto Dance Theatre with all the right qualifications. He had a PhD in mathematics, was well-connected, and he was an experienced lobbyist with access to the funding networks.

Dr. Jones was also charismatic, charming, and enthusiastic.

Jones was full of ambition for the company. In terms of modern dance, he felt, "Toronto Dance Theatre *was* modern dance in Canada. The company was *IT!*" He also knew that it was time for the company to heighten its profile and that, in order to accomplish this, it would need more money and more tours. He enthusiastically proposed his ideas to the artistic directors and they embraced his sense of excitement and his plans. Finally they had found somebody who could handle the business end of their company.

Jones joined the company with the title of managing director and a seat on the board of directors. For the other members of the board — Peter, Trish, and David — Roger's skills and drive meant they now saw themselves truly free to do the creative work they were interested in and to not have to concern themselves with the business aspect of running a dance company and school. They would no longer have to worry about the operational side of things: enrollments and curricula, studio scheduling, arranging bookings, paying salaries and bills. Jones' administration would take care of everything. Trish, not a domestic woman, knit Jones a tie in appreciation

Jones attempted to amalgamate the founders' visions and to create an image of a successful dance organization at the forefront of its field. In order to establish Toronto Dance Theatre as a major modern dance company, it needed financial backing. He talks about how he saw things:

> I took a hard look at where the funding was coming from. I think one of the early things I tried to do was to improve the operating funding both from the Councils and the private funding.... I got heavily involved in the Councils and became a major player on the

arts advisory panel of the Canada Council and other boards across the country.... A lot of [company] image stuff for me was on the financial side. I spent a huge amount of my time talking to Councils, talking to donors, simply getting money. Money was a big pre-occupation. My constituency, unlike theirs [the founders was] the corporations and the Councils.

As part of his "constituency," Jones became the treasurer on the board of the Dance in Canada Association.

Roger Jones had complete control of the financial and business aspects of the company. David remembers, "After [he] arrived, Peter, Trish, and I never wrote a cheque. We may have signed the cheques but we never put the amount or who the recipients of the cheques were.... We couldn't have traced the validity of every cheque we signed." This admission indicates the trust given Jones by the founders. It also is an indication of the tremendous sense of relief they felt at having someone who knew what to do and appeared to enjoy doing it, at the helm. For the next nine years, Jones was the captain and navigator of Toronto Dance Theatre and the founders were free to return to what they saw as central to themselves and for the company: creating, teaching, dancing, and supervising the artistic programming.

The Western Gamble

The democratic ethos of the artistic atelier (or, perhaps more appropriate for the times, artists' commune) was shifting towards institutionalization. If an extensive tour was to be undertaken, plans *had* to made *and* adhered to. The need for structure marked the beginning of a new period for the company.

Jones quickly involved himself in all aspects of the operations, including budgets. Plaxton, recognizing that Jones wanted to do more, gradually eased himself out but, before leaving the company, he helped to plan the first tour of the Western provinces in January 1974. This was the company's biggest touring gamble. With little support from any funding bodies, TDT made all the arrangements, renting theatres in five major cities. The tour was a triumph, garnering rave reviews and selling out 85% at the box office.

The School

Back on home ground, other elements of Toronto Dance Theatre were being restructured. The school officially advertised itself as a school for training in the Graham technique. Courses were geared more towards serious students of dance. Wives in need of exercise, and parents looking for an alternative to ballet classes for their children, could still come to the school but there was a distinct shift in emphasis towards serious training. Regular attendance at all levels of classes, which before had been on a "come when you can" basis, was strongly encouraged, but collecting fees continued to be a major challenge. The administration of the school was "too free" as Donald Himes, then-principal of the school, reflected in an interview with *Dance in Canada* in 1977.

> People would take a class without paying. We suffered from that climate of the sixties where everything was "Get in there and do your own thing, man." But you really can't train yourself for a career in dance that way.... It was very hard on the teachers, this casual attitude. With some students coming twice a week and others coming once a month.

The arrival of Marie Marchowsky from the Graham School in New York to co-direct the school with Donald Himes, marked another shift towards establishing a more formal protocol, as did the move into a larger studio space at the Finnish Community Centre on Broadview Avenue in December 1974. Everything was becoming more "professional."

Professionalism and (Sniff) "Amateurs"

The buzz word, "professional" was used to separate the technically adept dancer, the more experienced choreographer, and established dance company, from the younger dance companies and performance dance artists who were working with other media, exploring the effects of everyday movement and theatrical genres as a feasible part of dance expression. These artists were experimental, sometimes self-indulgent, and often limited in technique and training. But, for all that, their work was attractive to audiences in search of the "cutting edge." "There was a lot of other things percolating," says Peggy Baker, "like performance art people.... A lot of it was irreverent ... People who had more experience were seeing this stuff, these growing pains and these juvenile outbursts and thinking, 'You guys are just a big waste of time' but, in fact, we all have to go through this."

These times were hard for the company. They were not getting the houses they used to, and they had to defend their work and their teaching to the dance community and to the critics. By 1976, Marie Marchowsky left the organization over teaching issues. Donald Himes followed. He explains:

> We had tremendous battles about the Graham technique.... David went off on his own and had his own take and evolved. I didn't like some of the stuff he was doing. Eventually that is why I left; it [being the principal] was a part-time job for me. I was doing a million things. I came to a time where I thought, "I value this friendship more than these constant battles going on about what should be taught, [and] how it should be taught at the school."

Peggy Baker adds, "Those were down years for TDT ... the critics were slamming them, they couldn't get people out to their concerts — a lot of funky, funky stuff was happening."

Grant Auditions

Funding was readily available from the Canada Council but, as they do today, people applying for grants had to go through an audition process. Unfortunately at that time it was ballet people auditioning modern dance people. Trish recalls a time when a group of students (Pat Miner, Peggy Baker, Cornelius Fisher-Credo) were preparing for an audition; they returned feeling so intimidated because the class was held in the big studio at the National Ballet School. The rough wooden floor was covered in rosin and the barefooted dancers all got slivers and splits in their feet. Trish telephoned Monique Michaud, then dance officer of the Canada Council, to express her concerns that the modern dancers were being treated like second-class citizens and, besides, "How would they [ballet dancers] know how to evaluate these dancers?" When Peggy Baker did not receive a grant,

Peter Randazzo sprang to her defence. Peggy states, "It's a good thing he did because I got the grant." The fact that the founders were listened to suggests that the government agencies respected their experience and saw them as "senior artists" in the dance community.

Becoming senior artists may have had its rewards for the founders, but the infighting in the dance community undermined their position. Their own students were rebelling, wanting to do their own thing and find their own way. When that happened there was a tendency to regard everything they had done before as "crap." As Peggy Baker explains it, "TDT *was* the only modern dance centre in this city for awhile — so when people felt it wasn't a good place for them to go [to study], there was some frustration [on the part of the students]." Graham Jackson, writing of that period in his ten-year retrospective for *Dance in Canada*, picks up on that feeling, noting, "... more disheartening is the betrayal by TDT's old faithfuls. 'They're not doing anything new. It's just the same old stuff,' they complain, as though dance technique were something like a hat or an automobile that you could exchange for a new model every year." The frustration, familiar to most parents of teenagers, was new to the founders and difficult for them to understand.

Lightning Does Not Strike Twice: The Second International Tour

By the summer of 1974, the company was in London. But this time the Gods were looking elsewhere. In retrospect, Peter recalls that all the signs not to go were there, but they did not heed the warnings. The councils, concerned by the huge financial outlays, were lukewarm; there was difficulty with the transportation of the sets; David was still recovering from a bout with hepatitis. The day before they were to leave, Trish was rushed to hospital for emergency surgery. The programme had to be adjusted and apprentices and company members would have to take on roles for which they were inadequately prepared. It was not until they had reached England that the founders learned that the Sadler's Wells Theatre was not sponsoring the company's appearance as they had been led to believe and that, by default, they would have to undertake their own promotion. It was always Trish who had the ability to forge ahead in a crisis, and this tour, especially, could have done with her clarity, strength, and fortitude.

When the company arrived, they were greeted by a
hostile cultural ambassador who coldly informed them
that he had already written to the company that it was a
poor time to come. Whatever the reasons for ignoring his
communication and the cause of his prescience, he was
right. Something was very different from the first time
they danced in London — perhaps it was the venue itself
— more upmarket than The Place Theatre where they
had danced in 1972 — and very firmly attached to a long
tradition of classical ballet. The audiences were insulted
at the sight of these barefoot colonial upstarts on their
hallowed Saddler's Wells stage. And a sight it must
have been. Jones recalls
the performance of Earle's
Atlantis on opening night:
"The dancers were not
used to a raked stage ...
spears were dropped and
rolled all over the stage,
cues were missed.... It
was a disaster."

The Company was
savaged by the Eng-
lish critics and, in the
long-established tradi-
tion of national self-
flagellation, the Ca-
nadian Associated
Press reported the
news to its subsid-
iaries. Variations of
damning articles
appeared in papers
across the country, docu-
menting the slamming the company
received with loud headlines: "Critics Pan Toronto Dance
Theatre," and " 'Dull, tasteless, lumpy, contrived': Critics
stomp on dancers." The founders were devastated. The
company was now deeply in debt and the damage to their
reputations is something from which David feels they
never fully recovered:

> We were horrified [by the experience and the
> reviews]. Then we found out we couldn't pay
> for it and the season was disastrous. So it
> was Peter, Trish, and David who were irre-
> sponsible and internationally shunned for this

horrible and irresponsible thing we'd done at the Sadler's Wells. In fact, we [had gone] believing that we were being produced by the theatre as part of their series.

The performance in Angers, France, was well-received but, by then Peter was suffering form hepatitis and had to be carried offstage. In Lisbon, the Gods had turned their faces away again. The employees of the theatre were on strike but came in to watch the rehearsal. Afterwards, each dancer was presented with a red gladiolus. No one realized that the flowers so proudly carried were the symbol of the Portuguese Communist Party until the "violent and public curses" of the good citizenry alerted them that "this charming gesture" had another purpose. It was good to come home — or so they thought. On their return, they discovered that their Lombard Street studio was about to be taken over by the local squash club, but, in point of fact, it never was.

The archives do not record the success or failures of the subsequent North American tours but the budget of $70,000 for the European component had doubled. The company was in deeper debt than it had ever experienced; the founders' reputations as dancers, choreographers, and administrators in tatters. Everything went under the microscope to be examined by critics, funding agencies, and the financial community; all was found wanting. Missing from all the reports is any mention of Roger Jones, managing director and "impresario" of the second international tour. It was Peter, Trish, and David who were reported as fiscally and artistically irresponsible.

Suiting up

The failed English tour was one of the reasons that the advisory board was encouraged to take on a more active role in the operation of the company business. Peter Randazzo tells the story about Louis Applebaum, chairman of the Ontario Arts Council, not wanting to give him a cheque. "He said, 'I want to see someone in a suit.' I said, 'I'll put a suit on.'" "The next thing we knew," David continues, picking up the story, "we had a [proper] board." The duties of the advisory board were flexible and informal and with no clear lines of authority. "They [the founders and Jones] didn't want that. They weren't that kind of people," remembers Clifford Beatty, but they were expected to be aware of what was going on. According to Peter, Roger held all the financial information files at his home and provided the board with figures when the need arose. Despite this unusual managerial practice — there is no documentation to substantiate Peter's account — Roger was doing his job and allowing them the freedom to do their work.

Creating the Work: Two

Peter continued his explorations of psychological conflict. *Figure in the Pit*, inspired by the Edgar Allen Poe story, was made to a blood chilling score by Ann Southam. Graham Jackson wrote that Ann Southam "has always seemed especially sensitive to Randazzo's kinetic language, his wit, his violence." *Nighthawks*, inspired by the painter Edward Hopper (Peter would return to animate the work of Hopper twice more in the future) was, for William Littler, too repetitive: "*Nighthawks* makes its points and then repeats them, running the risk of turning the mysterious into the obvious."

In 1975 as a response to the growing charges of the work being too "heavy," Peter offered *L'Assassin Menace* to offset the growing complaints. Inspired by the surrealistic painting of René Magritte, Peter utilized the central criminal character, Fantmas, to reverse human values. This was a glorious success, in part, due to Peter's performance. Karen duPlessis remembers:

I don't think I ever missed a rehearsal of it in a theatre because I liked watching Peter do the tango. I would melt in my seat every time. He would come out on stage with such dark, mysterious maleness ... he was unbelievable! When Peter did *L'Assassin* you really wondered, "is he living this?'" You just questioned the depth of his intensity ... how deeply he [went] into the role.

In *Mythic Journey* and *The Letter*, Peter created two darker works, in response to which John Fraser observed, "... Randazzo does not push any solutions or answers on his audience. What he offers instead is the clear eyes of a perceptive observer of life."

This clarity of observation was evident in *Recital*, in which Peter took on the artificiality of etiquette, particularly as used by the patrons of the arts. Melodramatic and full of satirical touches, Peter uses classical ballet to both mock and represent the manners of the elite. The work reflects his diabolical sense of humour. He seems to be saying if we go down, let's all go down laughing. *A Simple Melody* was a romp of a different kind, a pursuit of a simple melody from a Gregorian chant to "Paddlin' Madelin Home." In it, he "takes swipes at high fashion, sexual role playing, classical ballet, and pop sentimentality ... but it is never belligerent." In this work in seven parts, there are two sections which pay homage to his Graham years and reveal a softer, more lyrical (and personal) choreography.

The work that David created in this period also attempted to address the audience's desire for "lighter entertainment." *Bugs*, a work in four parts, was a "a biological survey of behaviourism found in certain species of insects, revealing patterns not unfamiliar to certain animals." It brought the desired chuckles but Donald Himes recalls it as being rather silly and not indicative of David's ability as a master choreographer.

The master choreographer re-emerged with *The Faure Requiem* which David created for the Metropolitan United Church in Toronto, a work that was performed in religious settings and not in theatres. In *Mythos*, David explores the Greek saga of Phaedra from the woman's perspective, on a grand scale. David writes eloquently about the work, offering a glimpse of his personal philosophy:

Phaedra's crime is her choice of lovers.... Her
sorrow is lust — which even today can seem
... to be a trick of fate — a joke the gods can
play on us ... the insatiable physical longing
for someone who does not Love Us — cannot
Love Us[sic].... Times are changing, women
can now confess to such strong needs without demeaning their character. It is time to
reconsider Phaedra.

The struggle with lust, the longing for love, and the recognition of a higher force permeate David's work. "David
is a nineteenth century soul; he is a romantic; he makes
suffering creative," Trish remembers.

Recovering from her surgery Trish was unable to
dance or choreograph. She was, however, a forceful presence in the programming through her earlier works. The
revivals provided excellent opportunities for other dancers
to make her choreography their own and for audiences to
appreciate the power and intensity of her language.

TDT was a company representing the three founders'
work, new and old but throughout its history the company's choreographic workshops had given the company
members a place to experiment. Not only was this a supportive decision but it also meant that there was the possibility of finding new work to augment the repertoire. If
works were strong. they were taken on tour and given

exposure. Barry Smith had work presented as did Donald Himes, musician Ricardo Abreut, and old friend, Danny Grossman.

Danny

Danny Grossman, who knew the founders when they were all in New York studying, arrived in Toronto in 1973, to work at TDT as a guest artist. A short time later, in addition to his commitments at TDT, he joined the York University Dance Department as an instructor. Danny had been a dancer with the Paul Taylor Company, but he found little time or encouragement to create his own dances and he wanted to choreograph. His relationship with his old friends at TDT was unique. He performed as a member of the company but he also worked outside the organization. Toronto Dance Theatre functioned as an umbrella to facilitate his work and enable him to develop as a choreographer and gain a reputation independent of TDT. As Graham Jackson puts it, "Although the association has been a mutually satisfying one, they have never really influenced one another's work. Grossman has consciously sought a unique movement vocabulary, honouring no one, while TDT has continued to honour the Graham sensibility."

In 1975, while teaching at York University, Danny created *Higher* to the music of Ray Charles. *Higher* is a work of sustained athletic strength, performed by a man and a woman on a ladder; their relationship is explored as they crawl, slither, and slide up and down a ladder, rarely using their hands. The audience was intrigued and delighted and the piece was taken into the repertoire of

TDT. As an instructor at York University, Danny was able to explore compositional works with his students; *National Spirit* was created for these students and re-mounted for Toronto Dance Theatre. For Danny, 1976 proved to be a choreographic boon year. Besides *National Spirit*, he created *Triptych, Fratelli*, and *Couples Suite*, and now had five works in the performance repertoire of Toronto Dance Theatre.

The 1977–78 season was to be Danny's last with the company; he had enough work to make up a programme and was interested in pursuing his choreographic vision independently. In March, TDT divided into two groups: Toronto Dance Theatre travelled to the Maritimes for a three-week tour, while Danny took his group (which included TDT apprentices) to New York for a week of performances at the American Theatre Lab. Danny's group returned to Toronto for three informal appearances at the David Mirvish Gallery, before the two companies parted amicably. It had been a valuable association on both sides.

The Times They Are a 'Changin'

In searching for a metaphor to describe the Toronto Dance Theatre of this period, the computer screen saver comes to mind. The frame is constant and there is a recognizable stability, but the colours and patterns are continually changing. Barry Smith had left TDT in 1975 to work with the Martha Graham Dance Company and Kathryn Brown — with the company since 1972 — was now working independently while maintaining her affiliations with the company. David Wood, Sara Pettitt, and Helen Jones were preparing to leave. In 1976, Claudia Moore, Dennis (René) Highway, and Chuck Flanders joined the company. Chuck was a seasoned professional with a strong ballet background who came to TDT from Winnipeg Contemporary Dancers; Dennis Highway who began his training at the Royal Winnipeg Ballet, had gone on to study for four years with the founders of TDT. The exquisite Claudia Moore had left the National Ballet of Canada, performed with other companies, and studied with Lindsay Kemp in London. She spent some time training in the Graham technique at TDT's school before taking her place in the company. Suzette Sherman had apprenticed for two years with Winnipeg Contemporary Dancers, but she was not strongly trained in the Graham technique so she, too, joined the school. Of the attitude and training atmosphere, Suzette comments:

Community was integral to the fabric of the organization. TDT was a place you went to after you knew what it was you wanted to do. You knew why you were going, the choice to go was a conscious one, it was a distilled decision. TDT was a life affirming place, you did not have to be wooed or convinced to go.

The addition of these dancers to the company continued the tradition of school-trained dancers graduating into the company.

The association with York University and government Local Initiative Programs (which made it possible, among other things, for young artists in training to present themselves to the public) had provided a wider pool of talent from which to draw, while raising audience awareness and invigorating the dance scene generally. New dancers were joining a company with a past and the choreographic works that had lasted were those that accommodated numerous interpreters. When a role was reassigned in a revival, it bore the dancer's own individual stamp. The infusion of new dancers affected the nature of TDT itself: the "hippy commune" atmosphere was shifting to one of a family, built around the small core of seasoned dancers and the founders, to nurture the constancy of purpose. In 1976, dance critic Michael Crabb gave his impression of how the company operated:

> A kind of happy but very efficient anarchy exists within the company, ruled over with tolerant good humour by Roger Jones, a Doctor of Philosophy in Applied Mathematics who is devoted to Toronto Dance Theatre and has been its manager for four years. Although the superficial impression is one of disorder, the company seems to work best with a flexible internal organization. Jones is aware of all the plans that have to be made far ahead for fund-raising and touring; he also knows that the directors are not long-range planners. There are fights but a way has been found to comprehend the artistic freedom demanded by the directors with the organizational imperatives forced on the company by the need to survive.

On surer footing, TDT forged ahead.

The Toronto Dance Festival of 1976

To celebrate and promote the diverse dance activity that was now taking place in Toronto, Roger Jones, as part of his duties with the Dance in Canada Association, organized *The Toronto Dance Festival* at Toronto Workshop Productions theatre. For five weeks in November and December of 1976, works were presented by Dancemakers, Danny Grossman, Kathryn Brown, Judy Jarvis Dance and Theatre Company, Toronto Dance Theatre, and performance artist, Margaret Dragu. The proceeds from the opening performance were donated to the Dance in Canada Association.

Although listed separately, Danny Grossman and Kathryn Brown were actually working as guest artists with Toronto Dance Theatre. What is most interesting about this festival is the interlacing of dancers in each other's pieces. In Danny's work *Triptych*, the founders are the performers, and Peter and Trish are in the cast of David's revival of *Boat, River, Moon*. Trish also appears in Kathryn Brown's solo, *Waiting*. The festival programme is a marvellous document indicating who was actively part of the dance scene at this time; it also conveys a strong sense that TDT is the senior company in this intense period of dance activity. The celebratory atmosphere of a cohesive and supportive Toronto dance community engendered by the festival did not last for long.

In 1977, in recognition of their contribution to the growth of cultural facilities in Canada, Roger Jones, Trish Beatty, and Peter Randazzo received the Queen's Silver Jubilee Medal from Governor General Jules Léger. That David Earle was not recognized at this time is astonishing. There is some perception that his firm and rather outspoken questioning of the authority of the Canada Council vis-à-vis the role of the artist, may have been a factor. These honours confirmed the regard in which Toronto Dance Theatre was held, not only by the dance community but by the community at large.

By the mid-seventies, thanks to Roger Jones' efforts, Toronto Dance Theatre was receiving substantial financial support from the Canada Council but such generosity contributed to a growing unrest between the greater artistic community and the Canada Council. What was in question was the means by which the assessment process was conducted. There was a perception of backroom deals and luncheon agreements made and suggestions that some people fitted rather too comfortably into the pockets of others. The size of TDT audiences and the relevancy of its work in relation to the amounts of grants was queried. There is, of course, no evidence that TDT had ceased to be relevant (despite the British critics during the 1974 tour) nor that any deals were made. But everyone "knew" what was going on.

"... Authority Patterns Are Like Child-Parent Roles"

At the Dance in Canada Conference in 1977, the underlying unrest erupted and a confrontation occurred. The "silver seven" — the National Ballet School and six companies (of which TDT was one) which were heavily funded by the Canada Council — were forced to defend the large grants they received. It is interesting, in view of the changes that occurred after the conference, that the seven cited "professional development" as the reason for their greater share of funding. Peggy Baker, who includes herself as one of the "upstarts" she talks about, offers her analysis of the situation:

> I think partly what happened there (and this can only be part of it), was [that] there were people who had a lot of important experience and background, like Rachel Browne and TDT, but their upstart students who wanted to do something different, were starting companies maybe naively thinking that they were peers, which at the time they wouldn't have been. A lot of things were said.... We thought the generation that was in power was full of it, full of themselves and totally misled. What was really awful was that they [TDT] were coming from a time of being *very* highly respected and being the only game in town, to being undeservedly dumped on by their [own] students.

The conference marked the split between the "haves" and the "have nots." The founders, busy teaching and making dances, did not realize that the level of resentment was so great. At the conference, Roger Jones, resigned as acting treasurer of the Dance in Canada Association. Soon after, he was an organizing member of the Canadian Association of Professional Dance Organizations (CAPDO), setting professional dance companies apart from other dance activity in the Dance in Canada Association. This then raised another question, what constituted a professional dancer?

"... And Not Interfere Artistically"

The explosive 1977 conference was a blow to the spirit of dance across the country. The dynamics within the Toronto Dance Theatre company were also beginning to shift. Jones felt that the company needed stronger visionary leadership and he began to "meddle" in artistic decisions. Without consulting Peter, Trish, or David, he planned posters, decided what works would be presented, when seasons would occur, and the type of public relations material that the company would produce. Jones explains: "We had tremendous rows over things publicity said ... they [the founders] had a purist approach to publicity. [It] had to express explicitly philosophical

statements they chose to make.... There is a difference between 'P.R.' copy and the heartfelt angst of an
artistic director." His interference began to cause conflicts
between himself and the three founders, especially on the
issue of artistic programming. Roger wanted more "accessible works" and what he considered a more "balanced"
programme, but the founders had always worked from
inspiration, not for innovation. They did understand what
Jones was saying and, in reviewing the works of the
period, it is clear that they (Peter especially) did respond
with a number of choreographic "crowd pleasers" and,
according to Peter, "saved the company."

"Ever at the Mercy of Landlords"
The need for crowd pleasers which would attract (it
was hoped) a much wider and more numerous audience,
was manifestly evident by 1978 when the accumulated
deficit reached $138,316. The deficit was a result of the
extensive touring schedule, the rising costs of productions,
and venue rentals at home. The deficit was increased by
Jones' ambition and separate vision for the future of the
company.

Throughout its lifetime, Toronto Dance Theatre and
its school had been looking for a permanent home with
space for growth, performance, and storage. For the
founders, a home with adequate space was a dream.
Jones went after the dream. He felt that the company
was "ever at the mercy of landlords" and that, in order to
receive financial backing from businesses and corporations, the company needed something tangible, something
that indicated its stability. A building would demonstrate
to the surrounding community that Toronto Dance Theatre was a permanent and recognized national institution.

David discovered St. Enoch's Church on Winchester
Street in the heart of Toronto's Cabbagetown and brought
the others to see it. It was just what the doctor (and the
founders) had ordered. Cabbagetown has an illustrious
reputation in downtown Toronto. It is a haven in the
middle of the city. The oldest cemeteries and adjacent
park systems encompass its parameters, and St. Enoch's
and many of the Victorian houses and duplexes in the
area, have been designated as historical sites.

There is an ancient and direct connection between
dance and religion through its ritualistic elements and a
physical as well as mental devotion to something ethereal
and otherworldly. Where the altar of St. Enoch's church

once stood is where centre stage would now be situated, adding another level of spiritual connection for many of the dancers. Although what follows could hardly be described as a "miracle," there is, considering the difficulties, something miraculous about the survival and continuing achievements of Toronto Dance Theatre. As for Cabbagetown and TDT no divine intervention was needed, the company loved the area from the start and the Cabbagetown community soon came around.
They appear in full force every September when TDT opens its doors to all of Toronto for the Cabbagetown Tour of Homes.

Roger Jones made it possible for TDT to have a home. It would, he realized, take a year of extensive fund-raising and hard negotiations with both the federal and provincial governments to raise the needed money to purchase and renovate the church. He was prepared to place all his energies towards the acquisition; ongoing operating plans, maintenance and repair, and a capital improvement fund could be dealt with later. Both the Canada Council and the Ontario Arts Council advised against the outlay of a large amount of money at a time when a recession appeared imminent and the company was already financially overextended. But Jones ignored the advice.

The Tenth Anniversary

In 1978, Toronto Dance Theatre celebrated its tenth anniversary in style at the Royal Alexandra Theatre with two evening performances. Impressively, TDT shared the run with Merce Cunningham and his dance company from New York City. Each evening featured revivals of *Recital* and *A Simple Melody* (Peter) and *Atlantis* (David); *Courance*, a new work by David, completed the programme. The "Alex" was a beautiful old theatre (even before its stunning restoration in the 1980s) and a long way from the performance venues of the early days of TDT. The journey also affected the ways in which the founders had changed. In an article by Stephen Godfrey in *The Globe and Mail*, David answers the question about the style of the company, saying that it was no more than "the consciousness of not sticking to one style." He agrees ("with a smile"), that things are "looser" now and that, "For the first few years, you feel God is speaking directly through you. You dare not change anything you've done. Sooner or later, of course, you realize God is letting you do everything on your own."

In the same article, Peter comments on his work and his feelings about the company "I look at some of my earlier choreography with a shudder; it's so heavy, I can't believe it. Some of the dances are incredibly dark and gloomy, they really go over the edge ... I don't think a dance company should be a family; it should operate efficiently. You can't pay the rent on dreams and hopes."

Just after the 1976 festival, Trish had withdrawn from active participation due to a physical deterioration of the left side of her body. She was seeking therapy in the Alexander technique, which would influence her work in the future, but it was two years before she was able to dance or choreograph. Still, in retrospect, it is unusual and not a little sad, considering the strengths and skills of available interpreters, that none of her work was represented in the anniversary programme. Reflecting on those first ten years, Trish mused:

I felt I was able to give Peter and David strength and confidence to take our vision out in the world when they needed it, and they taught me how to listen to other people. So it was very important that we were together; there is no question it was fated. It wasn't easy. David always said ... there was always one person that was up when things were rough. Fate may have knocked two of us down, but there was always one who was up. It was a momentous task. There is no doubt that this was a collective journey.

The "momentous task" was about to get even harder, as efficient operation, artistic control of the programming, and creative bookkeeping in order to pay the bills, were to be big future issues. But the last words for this period must be David's:

I feel we've barely begun. We have a large space with a wooden floor now and sixteen disciplined people to deal with — everything else is icing on the cake.

4 Keeping Company

In 1979, besides the founders, only Susan Macpherson, who had been with the company since its inception, and David Wood, who had joined TDT in 1971, were company originals. They were the links that bridged the years and Susan, as the most senior dancer, was the mother figure for the incoming dancers. The seasoned dancers in the company were Nancy Ferguson, Claudia Moore, David Wood, Charles Flanders, and Wendy Chiles. Robert Desrosiers had just joined the company and David Hochoy was guesting from New York. Both came to TDT as experienced artists, having performed extensively elsewhere. Experience in other working conditions led them to question TDT's policies: Why didn't TDT have union conditions? Why weren't they dancing in larger houses? Why not have guest choreographers? The concerns of the senior dancers were offset by the enthusiasm of the junior members, Sherry Lanier, Karen duPlessis, Grace Miyagawa, Suzette Sherman, Jeannie Teillet, Mitch Kirsch, and Christopher House.

Christopher joined the company in 1979, at a tumultuous time in its history. The outlay of time and effort involved in the purchase and renovation of the new home left Jones little time to manage the company and the

"... all the sweet green icing's flowing down"

"MacArthur Park"
— a popular song of the 1970s

School as he had once done. Fund-raising and bookings fell off, leaving a cash-flow problem. Lack of money forced the cancellation of a season at the St. Lawrence Centre. Tensions within the organization mounted and in 1980, disheartened because of layoffs and bad press, four dancers left the company. The founders understood the dancers' reasoning. "They left for the same reasons I left Pearl Lang's company," says Trish. "Robert Desrosiers wanted his own company. Claudia Moore wanted to be with Robert. Nancy Ferguson became interested in theatre and film. We all have to move on to grow." This was especially true for Susan Macpherson. She wanted an opportunity to work with other choreographers, later joining the Danny Grossman Dance Company and developing an independent career as a soloist.

The timing of these departures directly reflected the company's financial instability as well as the pluralistic growth of modern dance, especially in Toronto. There were many in the arts community who felt TDT's devotion to the Graham technique held the company back from benefiting from developments of newer, more contemporary (and relevant) influences. These departures were noticed and the organization drew criticism from the press.

Keeping Three Balls in the Air

In order to facilitate the purchase of the building and reorganize the financial administration, Jones had decided to split the company from the school to create separate organizations. By doing this, the principal of the school could apply for separate public funding, thereby enabling it to have Professional Training Program status. By the end of 1979, Jones was managing three organizations: the Toronto Dance Theatre, the School of the Toronto Dance Theatre, and the Toronto Dance Foundation which Jones had set up in the founders' names in order to purchase St. Enoch's. Peggy Baker comments, "They [the founders] knew they had someone really good; he was that person they needed. He did the institution building that freed them up. Also it was probably the perfect scenario for Roger because they weren't in the office and they didn't know how to read a budget."

Despite the good intentions made after the disastrous English tour of 1974, the advisory board for Toronto Dance Theatre was still not sufficiently involved in the company. Clifford Beatty states that at this time, he was still "along for the ride. Roger planned everything." Jones supports Beatty's statement: "We'd done the whole thing. We'd raised the million and a half and we were in the building by 1979, but I must say that when the board finally became a board it was a good board. I had an enormous sense of relief that we had one. It was essential and long overdue." It is unclear if the board was aware of the $23,249 management salary drawn by Jones as the administrator of the Toronto Dance Foundation and separate from his Toronto Dance Theatre manager's salary, until after Jones' departure. However, it was Jones deepening involvement with artistic decision making that would be the reason for his leaving.

Creating the Work: Three

1979 marked Trish Beatty's return to the company and to choreography. There was a distinct shift in her choreographic focus:

Seastill was the first piece I did after two years of not dancing, not being able to dance. I wanted to see if I could just be beautiful and peaceful. That would be enough. *Seastill* isn't about human life, it was about the sea, which is part of where we have our life. I wanted to evoke the sea and all the sensuality and all the peace and all the beauty and timelessness that's down below.

Karen duPlessis recalls this work:

Trish is unlike anybody else [at TDT] where she doesn't work strictly to music, it provides more of the environment and you dwell within it. With her music, there are landmarks in the phrases that she uses loosely to be near. In *Seastill* the music was electronic and so ambient that it didn't matter which way you listened to it.... We were on tour and I don't know if the technician was paying attention, but the tape came on backwards and we had no landmarks that time, and we were the only ones who knew the difference.

Stephen Godfrey in *The Globe and Mail*, describes *Seastill* as "a mellifluous, nearly soporific work that, nevertheless, includes some finely observed movement of sea life and a sense of timelessness." For her followers, delighted to see her at work again, it was enough.

Trish's *Lessons in Another Language* (workshopped in 1979, presented in 1980) was applauded by the press and shows her return to form. Trish explains the process:

The first time we did *Lessons* it was called *Essay on*

Spanish Ideas, and it was conceived by Steve McCaffrey and me. We wanted to put something very intense and highly designed next to something very casual and impromptu and see what happened. We did it as if I was rehearsing my Spanish dance and he was the technician come to repair the tape recorder in blue jeans and an old shirt.... He bumped and banged across the stage and interfered with the music; he was very, very funny. The mistake was not putting Steve's name in the programme. So people were angry ... one member of the audience loudly demanded to know why someone didn't remove the "jerk" from the stage! The composer was also dismayed at what happened to his music, but he later gave me credit for having the "spunk" to do what I did.

"A delicious and ambivalent work ... such is the fine line Beatty treads between the serious and the comic.... She looked splendidly deadpan as the Spanish dancer while Earle was at his lobotomized best," wrote William Littler in his review of *Lessons in Another Language*.

"Lobotomized" is a word that could never be associated with David Earle as a choreographer and *Baroque Suite* is an example of his creative, searching mind at work. *Suite*, first danced in 1968 as *Mirrors*, had begun as David's homage to José Limón; other sections were added in 1972 under the new title. Originally, there were five parts to the work, set to the music of Pachelbel, Bach, Corelli, and Vivaldi. By 1973, *Baroque Suite* had taken on its final form, evolving into three sections, *Duet*,

Mirrors, and *Finale*. David reworked the piece in 1979 with a new *Finale* and new music. Alina Gildiner describes it as, "a work of filigree detail so elegantly wrought that the music rushes like air through the large spirals and slow sweeps of the movement ... no matter how often it is performed, *Baroque Suite* continues to display new moments."

This work is considered one of David's most inspired pieces of the seventies. Each section is full of eloquent moments, filtering the Graham technique through his own evolving, more fluid movement vocabulary. His knowledge is embodied in the work through images of paintings, patterns and manners of the Baroque era. *Baroque Suite* remains the most performed work in the history of the company. Following the success of the reworked *Baroque Suite*, David's Winchester Street Theatre solo evening, *Chiaroscuro* included the highly acclaimed *Frost Watch*, choreographed on a text by writer-poet Graham Jackson. *Exit, Nightfall* with its haunting conclusion, *Miserere* were presented in the early spring season of 1982 on tour in New York State.

Peter continued to work the vein of satire, using a humourous musical pastiche to create *The Light Brigade*. He also choreographed *Moving to Drumming* and *Duet Untitled*. Created for Sara Pettitt and Christopher House, *Duet* "represents," writes Littler, "a different Randazzo who peddled pain and exposure through so many early works. Set to a flagrantly romantic score by Michael J. Baker ... [the dancers approach] each other on a long diagonal, turning and balancing in flowing unisons in a way that could almost be called 'classical.'" Peter, no longer peddling his pain in his work, began to explore it in other ways. His choreographic output throughout the eighties would slow to a standstill.

It was young dancer Christopher House who would provide new material for the company's repertoire. He continued to dance but choreography increasingly became a complimentary means of his artistic contribution. David remembers how Christopher, who was living with him at the time, would move pennies around to facilitate his exploration of the relationship between group structures, "I still have a jar of pennies at home with all the names of the dancers in the company taped onto them." House's preoccupation with form is reminiscent of David's own days of creating button ballets.

For Christopher, like David, the manipulation of objects would pay off. His early works proved to be intelligent and thoughtful, with an underlying attention to the musical structure. *Toss Quintet* first appeared at the company's choreographic workshop in the spring of 1980. It highlighted Christopher's fascination with sharp, quick and complex movement, and sweeping use of spatial changes. It would be the first of many music visualization works that Christopher would choreograph and which would receive good notices from the Toronto press who clearly enjoyed his formalistic creations. *Toss Quintet* was adopted into the repertoire and in 1981, his talent as a choreographer earned him the title of resident choreographer.

"Christopher," says resident costume designer Denis Joffre,

> represented the newer dancers where technique was starting to push its way through. Emphasis on dancing was technical as opposed to theatrical. There was something about the physical presentation of [the Graham technique] in the work Christopher was starting to do both as a dancer and as a choreographer. I was part of that new momentum, that new look ... a period for TDT was closing and another one was starting.

Christopher recognized that these opportunities to dance and to create were made possible because of the founders belief in his talents and skill. He has never ceased to be grateful for their generosity and support.

Celebrating the New Decade

Together with the institutionalization of TDT, the seventies had marked the emergence of new, innovative dance companies and general expansion (with the attendant growing pains) within the dance community. By 1980, dance companies were ready to celebrate their growth, strength, and diversity. A historic performance characterized the camaraderie felt during this period — at least among the eight most senior dance companies in the country of which TDT was a prominent member. The Canadian Association of Professional Dance Organizations (CAPDO) organized a gala in May 1981 for the Opera Hall of the National Arts Centre, a theatre seating over 3000 people. Besides Toronto Dance Theatre, the invited companies were the Royal Winnipeg Ballet, Le Groupe de la Place Royale, Les Grands Ballets Canadiens, Winnipeg Contemporary Dancers, Anna Wyman Dance Theatre, Danny Grossman Dance Company, and the National Ballet of Canada. The event was titled *Gala*. TDT was asked to open with *Baroque Suite*. This long-standing favourite with TDT audiences brought the house down with its joyous freedom of movement and ferocious use of space. It was a triumphant performance for the dancers, for David, and for the Toronto Dance Theatre.

Un Certaine Âge

The achievements in the nation's capital moved the stakes to remain Canada's premiere modern dance company higher still. Pressures increased as other companies toured the circuits that had formerly been TDT territory. One way the company could continue to perform was to use their own venue, now called the Winchester Street Theatre. A series of evenings profiling the works of a single choreographer were held between September 1980 and February 1983. These repertory evenings were highly successful in terms of keeping the work before the eyes of the public but the theatre was not large enough to make a difference to the existing debts. Jones knew he had to find new venues and generate ideas, not only for developing audiences but for maintaining them in an increasingly competitive market. To help, Roger Jones hired General Arts Management Incorporated (GAMI) to market the company.

The relationship was costly and short-lived. GAMI reported to the board that TDT was a company that was not easy to sell. They explained some presenters wanted post-modern work, while others wanted guarantees that their "act" would fill the houses because they were not interested in supporting "fringe" events. GAMI cited the changing (and volatile) public taste and financial concerns as the primary reasons for their inability to book the company. At the end of their association with TDT, Peter Sever, president of GAMI wrote to Jones:

> It is apparent from the point of view of your artistic directors, they are doing the right thing artistically. They are creating the kind of dance and the kind of theatre which they believe to be right and true for their particular talent, tastes, and visions. I do not question their integrity ... but as ... artistic

directors of a major Canadian dance organization, they must listen to the realities which are offered them ... our clients pay us to give suggestions, raise questions, and think aloud together. The 'thinking aloud' process has, I feel been misunderstood by your artistic directors and has resulted in nothing positive at all....

This failure to communicate (on everyone's part) put the company further into debt and increased the tension between Jones and the founders which was already stretched to the breaking point. They felt left out because Jones, who was in charge of the renovations of the building, did not discuss the plans with them nor, they were beginning to sense, was he keeping them accurately informed about the financial situation. The founders did not learn the full financial status of the company or the school until Monique Michaud of the Canada Council, notified them that the school was $65,000 in debt. The news was the spur that engaged the interests of the founders and the board. The minutes of the board meeting of June 10, 1981, announced that Jones would be leaving the organization and the conditions of his departure suggest that people had some concerns about the double salary. The minutes state: "Roger is leaving in September but will continue to put in a twenty-hour week unsalaried. His main thrust during the summer will be fund-raising." The minutes add that the board will be responsible for hiring a new general manager whose primary responsibility will be to find bookings for the company and that "the Canada Council will only accept someone who has the 'right' qualifications."

A proposal was then sent to the two councils, together with the audited financial statement for August 1981 which reads, in part:

The theatre has experienced significant losses to August 31 1981 resulting in an accumulated deficit of $281,809 as at this date. The Theatre's continued existence as a going concern depends on its ability to obtain sufficient revenues to fund its operations and extinguish its bank loan and other liabilities.

Both councils warned that they considered the company to be in financial crisis. In September 1981, Edward (Ed)

Oscapella was hired on a letter of agreement with the now active board of directors, as general manager to "clean house."

The "Disaster Specialist"

In the eyes of the councils, Ed Oscapella was the consummate financial general manager and the perfect person to cope with the problems TDT faced. He sums up his purpose: "I make it [the company] work, then leave.... The reality of the financial situation and the cost of things means, in a crisis situation, you can't do everything.... My job was to get the company rolling and back on track."

Putting the company "back on track" meant an end to touring and performing in large venues. Oscapella also intended a thirteen-week lay-off for the company. He made two phone calls, one to Susan Cohen at the Ontario Arts Council and the other to Monique Michaud at the Canada Council. He informed the two dance officers that if the funding to the Toronto Dance Theatre was cut, the company would cease operations altogether. Both agreed to allow the funding to continue in order to enable the restructuring of the company.

The board did not want to take the lay-off action but Oscapella "forced the issue by paying outstanding bills until the money ran out." He then announced the company lay-off which saved over $100,000 in salaries alone. "Ed represented ... that sort of 'I'm going to make you pay attention to reality' by hitting you over the head with a hammer ..." Denis Joffre remembers. "He would literally walk around the building in his overalls and a hammer fixing stuff up in the church.... He was ... going to clean up our act.... It was necessary [but] in the creative end, we hated it because it meant our creativity was stifled."

Responding to the layoff, soloists with the National Ballet of Canada, Peter Ottman and Albert Forister raised over $900 to help TDT dancers meet living expenses and when the company returned to work in February 1982, performances continued only in their own small Winchester Street Theatre. As a public indicator of the new frugality, programmes no longer held the glint of professionally reproduced photographs but were photocopied pages folded in half. With Ed came financial stability but the interrelationships of the company was severely challenged. Trish says it "definitely was a rough period." The founders tried to be of help to Ed but, David remembers,

> Ed often didn't let us deal with our financial difficulties creatively. For example, I had this idea we should do a fund-raising thing with Bic's Pickles. We could get these huge pickle people to support us.... We'd go to Bay and Yonge wearing pickles and these signs that would say, 'Only a nickel gets us out of our pickle.'

Although they could laugh, the times were bleak. For Trish who shared a dressing room with David in the tower of the old church, they were in some ways, "the best years." "My poor darling brother was always trying to get us to have more meetings. Because we were never good at meetings (it's an administrative mind that can take meetings), we stayed very close.... [David] lived with Pete, so it kept that sort of interconnectedness."

Karen duPlessis sympathetically recalls that Peter was having a harder time dealing with the situation than David and Trish. "There was tension, the whole building was on tenterhooks ... you never knew whether something you said would trigger [Peter] off. And if you triggered him, you didn't want to be near him. [He was] just short of physical violence." "Often," Trish recalls, "David had to mediate and calm Pete down and he had to do that with a lot of people, not just me."

During Oscapella's tenure at Toronto Dance Theatre (1981–1983), he established accountability at the board level by making their meetings the place where final decisions were made, and he initiated operational procedures standard in other companies (for instance, the use of written contracts for dancers and staff). Oscapella also proposed a financial deficit reduction plan and put in place checks and balances regarding financial matters, for example, three people were now required to sign any cheque in excess of $2500. Michael Crabb summarized this transition period:

In the 1970s, the company helped trigger a modern-dance explosion across Canada. By the 1980s, however, it began to acquire a reputation as old-fashioned. While modern dance went in various new directions, ranging from contact improvisation to multimedia formats, TDT remained loyal to its Martha Graham roots. And it was saddled with financial problems after spending $1.2 million to buy and renovate historic St. Enoch's Church in Toronto's fashionable Cabbagetown. Its co-founders were, as Earle concedes, "burned out."

The founders were indeed disillusioned and tired. They were still responsible for creating new works, remounting old works, teaching, going to board meetings and giving interviews. As choreographers, they felt their creativity was threatened. At one point Ellen Busby, then stage manager and acting as the liaison between the artistic directors and the administration, had been sent into Ed's office to remind him TDT *was* a performing company. In an interview with Paula Citron for *Performing Arts in Canada* in 1983, Peter exclaimed, "It's taken me fifteen years to work my way down." David explained, "We just wanted to be choreographers and were forced into being bad administrators.... The three of us feel tortured and under constraints.... I think our growth was stifled by the arts councils who felt we had to stay at a certain level until other companies caught up." Trish felt they were too idealistic to be artistic directors in the sense that "always to program to please is not the artistic task, we just wanted to show the best work and the newest." The strain of running the company had taken its toll. All three needed time — time to concentrate on their health, to fulfill their personal goals for choreography, to focus on their teaching, and time to be free of the burden of administration hanging over them. They also felt it was time to pass the position of Artistic Director on to someone else.

A Pearl at Any Price: 1983–1987

David Earle's first student in Toronto resurfaced as a source of support. Since being a student at Three Schools of Art, Kenny had taken a degree at the University of Toronto while continuing to take classes with Trish and

David. He went on to dance with the Martha Graham Dance Company and the Alvin Ailey American Dance Theater. During the seventies, when he was with the Ailey company, Kenny returned to TDT to teach summer school courses. He had served as rehearsal director for the company's reduced touring schedule and, in the summer of 1982, David invited Kenny, Christopher House, and James Kudelka to work as choreographic collaborators on the Stratford Musical Festival's highly touted and successful opera, *Dido and Aeneas*. Kenny was a member of the family.

On David Earle's recommendation in August of 1983, Kenny Pearl became TDT's first non-founding artistic director. He was chosen, he felt, because of his long relationship with the founders. "They had been my teachers and a good part of my early inspiration." Kenny goes on to remember:

> When I arrived as a director, I was inexperienced. Many thought I would be just a mouthpiece for the founders.... As raw as I was, I knew I would have to find my own way.... For me the task of artistic director was to encourage the creativity of everyone in the building ... to treat people well and to present the company with pride.... My goal

was not to create a new vision but to stretch the one that was already there.... I felt that the presentation of the work and the perception of the company by audiences, critics, and arts councils had to change ... the entity called TDT needed a shot of confidence; a new belief in itself.

In summer of 1983, the founders joined Christopher House as resident choreographers and formed an artistic committee to give advice to the new artistic director.

In theory, the Artistic Advisory Committee would recommend a unified artistic direction for Kenny to implement. Kenny described these meetings as difficult because, "how could these choreographers have identical artistic expectations?" He quickly realized that he had accepted a post that was inherently between a rock and a hard place: the "rock" being the founders' various visions, the "hard place" a double-edged sword of financial accountability demanded by funding bodies and outside presenters' programming demands. The advisory meetings ceased after the first season when Kenny realized he had to find his own voice as artistic director. "I think when Kenny came on, he saw the potential of the company," says Christopher House. "Kenny just wanted to keep things vital and he wanted the work to be about the people in the company. He didn't want the dancers always wearing costumes with somebody else's name in the back."

With Kenny Pearl as artistic director, and Ellen Busby as administrator, the Canada Council and Ontario Arts Council assumed a "wait and see" position. Kenny had to learn the repertoire, teach class, and bear the burden of public expectations all at once. It was quite a task but the 1983–84 season proved to be a triumph for the company with new works like the magnificent *Painters and the Dance* (Beatty), *Glass Houses* (House), and *Court of Miracles* (Earle). The company excelled technically and proved itself to the councils. However, Kenny encountered a problem that would lead to misunderstanding, jealousy, tension, and his early dismissal in 1987.

Kenny tried to freshen the company's image, making it less austere and more appealing to the audience. He designed programmes that framed the works in a way that would present the full range of the company's dynamics to the public. While on tour to Vancouver in 1984, for the first time outside Toronto, the company devoted an entire evening to one choreographer, Christopher House, but the programme for the hometown season in January 1985 was shared by Earle, House, and Randazzo. In June 1985, at the Dance Canada Festival held at Brooklyn College in New York, four of the five works were choreographed by House, the fifth was choreographed by David Earle. In that same year, David had taken advantage of his sabbatical from artistic directorship and choreographed *Realm* in response to an invitation from Erik Bruhn, artistic director of The National Ballet of Canada. In 1986, both Beatty and Randazzo premiered new works, but the programmes usually presented only one of their works at a time, while House and Earle, would have more. This programming was no different from the seventies, when Peter's repertoire commanded the bulk of the programming. Busby defends this strategy:

> From my end as manager, we saw Christopher House as being a young talent and at that time being a relatively unknown [choreographer].... Kenny and I saw [his work] was a way to make Toronto Dance Theatre one of the items that would be 'Hot Stuff'.... From an organizational point of view, that's what we should have done because the company needed to look like a new company. From the founders' point of view, that was maybe not appropriate.... They saw talent in Christopher's work and were willing to give him an opportunity but it was still their company.

Programming emerged as the key point of contention between Kenny and the founders. Because illness left them unable to create, Trish and Peter presented Kenny with a list of works that could be revived so that they would be more widely represented on the programme. Kenny maintained that TDT should place its financial priority on new work over revivals. As time passed, it appeared to Trish and Peter that they were being relegated to founder status (a role that had not been defined by Oscapella and, indeed, one with which other Canadian companies have struggled). What they most resented was that they were not being involved in the artistic process of the company. The founders expected Kenny Pearl to take their advice, and when he did not, the loss of control was deeply felt. The problem of the interpretation of the title, artistic director, became an issue. The founders explained their view to Paula Citron in an article for *The Toronto Star* in 1987:

> Kenny was hired to be an agent for the four resident choreographers. Earle says "His job was to showcase our works and get them known to a wider audience as well as taking over administrative duties." Adds Beatty, "We didn't give the company up. We just put it into someone else's hands for a while ... we never intended to abdicate totally from artistic concerns. We thought that we would share and collaborate in planning programs. But Kenny was nervous about audience reaction to some of our work and he hesitated to schedule us, giving Christopher [House] the lion's share of the programming." Randazzo explained, "Kenny tried to make the company more commercially viable by building programmes that would have wide audience appeal. That meant that some of us were left out in the cold. But we created TDT — it's our baby and we felt the contributions of the senior people weren't being recognized.

Pearl sees the situation differently:

> During the four years I was at TDT, Trish and Peter only each created one piece [Peter's *Rewind* and Trish's *Radical Light*].... David continued to create with his startling consistency ... in answer to my critics, I stacked the deck with Christopher's work on only one occasion — the company's return to New York when I had specific demands from the producer.... I didn't favour a choreographer; I favoured excellent work.... I did at least eight revivals in the four years I was with them — that's not bad.

The founders believed that art should not have trends, all the works in the repertoire were good and they wanted the general audience to trust its own experience. The conflict between the founders desire to be more widely represented in the repertoire and the financial imperatives of survival in a competitive environment was, for the first time, clearly articulated during Kenny Pearl's artistic directorship. Despite the internal tensions and before embarking on tour with the company, he was encouraged to extend his contract.

After the "wildly successful" Mexican tour, the board made the decision to end Kenny's contract without any discussion with him. "When they asked if I could leave as soon as possible, they must have felt just a bit guilty ... [they] asked me not to talk to the press about what they were doing or how they were doing it." When the board asked for Pearl's resignation, he gave it freely, acknowledging that, "it was never my company. After fifteen years it was, understandably, difficult for the founders to watch someone with a new voice guiding their creation.... I always felt like a visitor in their house ... and I was always prepared to walk away."

Kenny Pearl's dismissal was not handled with the tact and consideration that he deserved, considering the strong steps forward the company had taken under his artistic directorship.

Creating the Work: Four

Although all the works in the repertoire were good, it is certainly clear that Christopher House was creating the "hot stuff" that was both crowd pleasing and artistically innovative. Many of the pieces remained in the repertoire, confirming that his creative invention was fresh and worth revisiting both for the dancers and for audiences.

Animated Shorts instantly became a signature piece that caught the attention of the Canadian dance world. Like many of Christopher's pieces, the choreography enlightened a complicated electronic score by Michael J. Baker and required dancers of great musicality. Karen duPlessis described her part in *Animated Shorts*:

> My part involved roaring out of the wings, into a space within the group, backing out again, and heading offstage. I always imagined I was a little sports car that drove into the garage, changed its mind, and headed out again. The audiences sometimes struggled with the opening movement of the piece, but the last movement, which was built on a progression of sevens, eights, nines, and a ten, was so fast and so uplifting, they were all but on their feet. The piece ends with a very

fast flip of every woman over partners' shoulder to a dead-stop finish on one count. There were a few times ... aaagh!

William Littler's review reflects duPlessis experience, "Inspired by the frenetic pace of animated films, *Animated Shorts* put high octane into Toronto Dance Theatre's tank."

Glass Houses, choreographed in 1983, would become one of Christopher's most famous early works. Ann Southam's score, "Glass Houses #5," not originally intended for dance, inspired Christopher to create a playful and athletic exploration of the joy of movement, parallel-

ing the music's construction and surprising the audience with the off-centring of formulaic patterns. Choreographed on three women and two men and designed by Denis Joffre, the work climaxes in a series of awe inspiring lifts where the female dancers seem to hover parallel to the ground for a brief moment. Anna Kisselgoff of the *New York Times* wrote, "*Glass Houses* showed Mr. House at his most exciting. Ann Southam's minimalist score ... is matched on stage by five dancers whose circling or chain patterns are starting lines for an incredible series of whipped turns." Like *Animated Shorts, Glass Houses* demonstrated Christopher's fascination with the musical form and dance's relationship to music. The piece won him the 1983 Jean A. Chalmers Award for choreography and propelled him into the international spotlight as a new and exciting Canadian choreographer.

In March of 1982, Peter's solo evening, *Dances of Randazzo*, was presented at the Winchester Street Theatre and included new works: *Octet, Enter the Dawn*, and *Arc*. The programme is remembered for the remarkable solo made on Sara Pettitt. The inspiration came, for the second time, from an Edward Hopper painting, "Morning Sun." In *Enter the Dawn* the dancer luxuriously lingered in balances that transmit both a physical and emotional message. The work accentuated the beauty of the female body and the incredible control of the soloist, especially in extended poses. Paula Citron described the work as a love poem to a female dancer. She read Peter's intentions accurately. In his words, "I love women, and this dance was a gift to one particular woman from a man who loved her."

By 1985, Peter's demons had caught up with him and he was struggling with alcoholism. Like many alcoholics he "didn't think [he] had a problem." His 1986 work, *Rewind*, was to be his last choreographic contribution to the company in the eighties, although he did works for Randy Glynn and Anna Wyman. Peter remembers the last half of the decade as being a vicious spiral into a mental hell, "I thought I was losing my mind." He lived in a nightmare state of mind and body; his mental, artistic, and spiritual outlook were skewed by an alcoholic haze. The explosion of new work and the momentum generated by Pearl, distanced him from the others. It became impossible for him go into the studio to create and he resented that all that was left for him was to teach. He had given his life to invent this company, surely it could provide for him when he needed it most?

For Trish, too, health issues were equally crucial. She was now in her late forties, "The forties are tricky for a dancer. It's very hard work — if you're complex at all." Although she was suffering from hypoglycaemia, it was a symptom of a deeper malaise. As Suzette Sherman remembers it, "Trish went through a huge transition coming to terms with not being the dancer she had once been. It's hard; she was trying to find out if she still fit, if she wanted to fit, or why she didn't fit." For Trish, it was more complex than that:

> I was going through a complete emotional, spiritual, and physical change. I realize I was approaching my life in dance from what I now call male values in the archetypal sense and it was damaging my body, in particular the left side. I have since found out [that is] is referred as to the feminine side, the side of feeling and flexibility. I was examining how I operated in the world and in my art form of dance. I was trying to find a new way of being in the world as a woman.

One way in which Trish attempted to bring all the components of her life into one statement was *Painters and the Dance*. The process of celebration began in 1979 when she received a senior arts award grant from the Canada Council. Her enormous colourful vision was an attempt to use choreography to express the life within the visual — the large abstract canvases of artists Gordon Rayner, Aiko Suzuki, and Graham Coughtry. *Seastill* (1979) and *Skyling*, (1980) were joined with two new pieces of choreography, *Emerging Ground*, and *Raptures*

and Ravings, to create the moving landscape of *Painters and the Dance*. The program was dedicated to "a future of peace and world union." The musical scores on which the choreography was built were by long-time TDT collaborators Ann Southam, Robert Daigneault, and Michael J. Baker. The event was a joyful collaborations between artists, dancers, and musicians in every sense of the word. In 1984, Trish received an Award of Merit from the City of Toronto for her pioneering work in the field of modern dance, and *Painters* was a contributing element to that award.

Painters and the Dance premiered at the St. Lawrence Centre in September of 1983 and from there went on to play at the National Arts Centre in Ottawa. Although everything appeared to go smoothly on opening night, Holly Small, one of the five additional dancers hired by Trish, recalls substituting for an injured dancer at the last minute:

> Originally, Patricia Beatty hired me just to dance in *Seastill*, a serenely beautiful dance that was wonderful to perform. My memory of *Raptures and Ravings*, on the other hand, is a chaotic blur. Just a few days before *Painters and the Dance* opened, lead dancer Grace Miyagawa was injured and I was asked to take her part in *Raptures and Ravings*. I had exactly one day to learn it and while Gordon Rayner's set of ramps and trampolines was a tempting playground, for me it was not fun. I remember my partner, Luc Tremblay, trying to coax me through a terrifying section where all the women had to stand to their full height on the men's shoulders and, with no visible means of support, appear completely at ease up there while the men walked about. I also remember two gigantic painted fans. Karen duPlessis and I had to crouch behind them and glide them about the stage. How I strained not to miss any of Karen's whispered cues as the monstrous band of artist/minstrels wheezed and honked past us. I remember on opening night, designer Denis Joffre arrived at the theatre without the top to my costume and I had to wear Suzette Sherman's sweatshirt. It was snug, long-sleeved and nearly the same

beige colour as the elegant silk thing he had fitted me with, nevertheless, I was mortified. And I remember at the reception afterward Christopher House commented, inexplicably, that mine was the only costume that fit properly. For me, *Raptures and Ravings* was the gruesome flip side to *Seastill* but now, fifteen years later, I think of it with particular fondness.

Except for one more work, the "highly charged and moving" duet, *Radical Light* (to the music of Carlos Chavez) in 1986, *Painters and the Dance* was Trish's last new contribution to the TDT repertoire of the eighties. It proved to the Toronto dance community that TDT could construct a monumental work on a grand scale and two months later, TDT mounted a Christmas production that would come to rival the National Ballet's *Nutcracker*.

In December 1983, *Court of Miracles* was first performed at the newly built Premiere Dance Theatre. David envisioned the event as an opportunity for all members of the dance community to work together to create an annual event for which David would act as director and principal choreographer. He constructed a scenario, based on the medieval happening that took place on the feast of St. Nicholas when all the roles of society were reversed: the rich changed places with the poor, the mad became the angels of God, and even the poorest "strove to have something to give to the forgotten." The idea was that David would invite different choreographers each year to invigorate the work to keep it fresh for both the dancers and the audience. The first choreographers were Peter Randazzo, Carol Anderson, Christopher House, and special guest choreographer, James Kudelka. In future years, David would continue to invite TDT alumni and old friends like Lilian Jarvis, Veronica Tennant, Lois Smith, Celia Franca, Danny Grossman, Lawrence Adams, Angela Leigh, Erik Bruhn, and others from the independent dance world, to perform. Often these guest artists appeared as one of the Seven Deadly Sins. (Trish remembers fondly being cast in the role of "Pride.") *Court* required a company of over fifty dancers and drew from the School of the Toronto Dance Theatre and Canadian Children's Dance Theatre to fill out the casts.

Court of Miracles would become a Toronto Christmas favourite for eleven years and has accumulated a wealth of stories. Penny Olorenshaw, long-time stage manager with TDT remembers:

Court of Miracles ended with a beautiful tableau of the asylum inmates-turned-saints climbing the ladder to heaven while bathed in a golden light; below them knelt the royalty, townsfolk and beggars who had witnessed the miracle. The curtain closed, then opened again, to reveal the tableau once more. The curtain closed again, the music started, and after the dancers rushed into their new places, the curtain opened again for the choreographed bow. At least that's how it was supposed to work.

One night the curtain closed and the music started. Suddenly I realized that the curtain had opened at the same time! The dancers were revealed with their backsides to the audience and they were rather shocked to discover that the curtain was no longer hiding them!

Karen duPlessis:

Getting to be the little sheep was the tenderest thing I've ever done, because I felt like the little children in the church doing the tiny Christmas pageants. It was like a little jewel, free of guilt, free of envy, free of anything except me and something that was heartfelt. That's why you dance, to get to that place.

David, tells the true miracle of *Court of Miracles*.

In spite of dancers' poverty, they are conscientious tippers. The waitress at the bar in

that Windsor Hotel told Ricardo Abreut that because of the generosity of the fifty to sixty people performing in *Court*, she would be able to make Christmas for her children for the first time in three or four years.

It was a miraculous production in many ways, not the least of which was the guaranteed annual revenue it generated.

During this first half of the decade, the company excelled, propelled by the great pieces such as *Court of Miracles*, *Painters and the Dance*, and *Glass Houses*, but none would reach the exposure or acclaim that *Sacra Conversazione* achieved. This work represented the accumulation of David's thinking, experience, musicality, spirituality, and creativity. The work was originally staged on the Festival Company at the Banff Centre for the Arts during the summer of 1081. Even when Kenny Pearl saw the poor quality rehearsal videotape that David showed him, he recognized that it was a perfect piece for TDT.

The work has its source in a visit to Paris. There, David witnessed a humble funeral procession arriving at the Cathedral of St. Denis, the casket bearing the inscription, "Pour Jean, 18 ans." Using this simple image, the work became an examination of the stages of grief and how, with the help of others, all tragedies may be overcome. During the rehearsal process, to help understand the tragedy and grief of war and loss, dancers explored imagery of people who were "disappeared" in the night, of loved ones found hanging, of the devastating rabble after a violent attack. Well received by the home audience, its

worldwide impact was phenomenal. Karen duPlessis remembers the huge audience in Mexico City, "the tears
running down their faces ... who here [in Toronto] has
had the experience of seeing your loved one hanging."
Michael Trent says of a later tour, "We had eight curtain
calls and people would walk out of the audience to give
us flowers.... It was as much an emotional experience for
us as it was for the audience ... this was in 1991 when
things were starting to change in Poland and the piece
spoke to them." Coralee McLaren, too, was deeply moved
by the audience members who came onto the stage with
tears in their eyes, presenting flowers and embracing
them. For David, successful as *Sacra* was around the
world, it was most truly understood by its South American audiences.

I think *Sacra* should represent a kind of triumph; it's really triumph of life over death

and the triumph of community, and the triumph of any peoples who feel themselves to
be secondary or persecuted in some way to
simply giving into persecution ... to fail to
meet the challenge. All those layers, I think,
exist in the piece, and I think when it was
danced in South America for people who
understood both political struggle and the life
and deathness of life, that it got the kind of
response that I believe I would want the
piece to have.

Sacra Conversazione would go on to be one of the
most successful signature presentations of the company. It
is ironic that the initial success of *Sacra* came during the
last tour to be arranged with Kenny Pearl as artistic
director.

5

David Earle: 1987–1994

In 1987, just before Pearl's departure, David and Christopher were the subjects of two half-hour documentaries called *The Dancemakers*. While these two documen-

taries marked the success of Toronto Dance Theatre and recognized the work of the artistic and administration staff, they also profiled the careers of the two men whose vision would guide TDT for the next ten years. It seemed, to Pearl, inevitable that the creator would miss his creation and that, after the time off "to refresh himself with outside projects and whatever," David would return.

David took over as artistic director in 1987 with the reluctant bless-ings of his co-founders. For him, it was a nat-ural step: "I've always been the moveable piece," he told Paula Citron in *The Toronto Star*. "I bend more

"... I always figured this reunion would take place sooner or later."

Kenny Pearl, 1998

easily than the others. When the three of us ran the company I did the programming because I was not a central dancer in my works while Trish and Peter were. I was the guy taking notes, so I guess I always was the unofficial artistic director...." Citron goes on to note that, "the Pearl legacy of marketing for audience appeal is not lost on David, grateful for the strong image of the company forged during the last four years."

At the same time as David's appointment, Ellen Busby, the general manager, decided it was time to leave but agreed to assist in the transition by remaining on staff for a few months. Ken Pierson took over from Ellen with expanded responsibilities and a new title: administrative director. Ken, an experienced manger with companies such as Dancemakers, Green Thumb Theatre, and Ballet British Columbia, had a deep love of the dance world. He was intense and businesslike and his style did not easily mesh with that of the David. "There are different kinds of leadership provided from the managers," Ken remembered in 1992. "Some people are very aggressive artistic leaders and others are very passive. At Toronto Dance Theatre it's very passive ... they'd rather let things happen organically, but unfortunately if you're planning two years ahead and you have to do grant applications and fund-raising ... it's no way to operate."

David took the advice of the other resident choreographers and to avoid conflict, he met with each person individually before arriving at a final decision. Trish and Peter trusted David to weigh their opinions carefully. The communication between David and Ken gradually eroded and the board of directors became the main liaison. "It was like having the carpet pulled out from under you, [Ken] didn't come to me.... I would hear from the board. So on a personal level, which is really quite important in a small arts organization, there wasn't much dialogue."

Ken Pierson recognized that the company was established to serve the resident choreographers. For him, the question was how to address the present and future needs of the institution without turning it into a bureaucracy and to nurture the choreographic energy which was the foundation of Toronto Dance Theatre. He set about preparing a five-year plan which incorporated the founders' existing long-term goals and that was, at the same, flexible and responsive to the creative nature of the people involved and to the changing market place. Pierson's extraordinary abilities to seize every opportunity allowed Toronto Dance Theatre to turn vision into reality. Trish explains, "He understood superbly the role of the artist. Ken brought style and stature to the company. He sent flowers and wonderful cards. He loved the dancers."

And none of this would have happened without an extraordinary company of dancers.

Golden Boys and Golden Girls

As in the past, dancers for the company were drawn from other places as well as the School of the Toronto Dance Theatre. As teachers in the school, the founders, and Christopher were able to spot and nurture talent as well as establish creative working relationships with these future professionals. Because seasoned company dancers also taught in the school, a high level of professionalism, a reverence for dance, and respect for the repertoire, was inherent in the training.

At the school, students learned pieces from the repertoire and participated annually in *Court of Miracles*. This exposure meant that dancers moving from school to company had an easy and comfortable transition. In 1986, five graduates from the school, Laurence Lemieux, Rosemary James, Sean Marye, Ron Ladd, and William Elias joined the company. Two years later, four more gifted students, Coralee McLaren, Graham McKelvie, Kate Alton, and Crispin Redhead were invited to join. The company became a uniquely blended ensemble of talented people. The technical level and emotional range

The School of The Toronto Dance Theatre

of the dancing, so greatly appreciated by critics and audiences, was a confirmation of the evolution of the Graham technique in Canada and an affirmation of the founders' unwavering commitment to their artistic vision.

Suzette Sherman characterized these times as the golden years of the company's artistic production. The dancers connected in a way that she had never experienced before. "We had been dancing together for so many years and we had a lot of trust for one another." Company members knew they could risk as artists and that someone would be there to catch them, literally and figuratively. Coralee McLaren recalls everyone laughing with each other and being able to "experiment her heart out" in the studio. Rosemary James, current rehearsal director and former dancer remembers:

> We were like a family unit; there was good energy, really positive artistically. David brought this to the company. [Other] people were always surprised ... because of the unity and the bonded feelings we had for each other.

The school prepared these dancers for professional careers but nothing could prepare them for the touring that lay ahead.

The 1988 twentieth anniversary year is characterized as a season on the road. To celebrate their longevity, the founders wanted to continue bringing dance to every region of Canada. They asked Ron Snippe, long-time lighting designer and tour manager for the 1988–89 season, to book Toronto Dance Theatre anywhere and everywhere across Canada. He did — from Sioux Lookout to Swift Current, from Medicine Hat to Hamilton, from Dryden to Weyburn; then overseas to Spain and Germany, and to Seoul, Korea, where TDT represented Canada at the 1988 Olympic Arts Festival.

For their contribution to the arts, the founders were given the Toronto Arts Award for Performing Arts. It was at this celebration that David made his statement, "For twenty years we have been making love to Toronto and for twenty years Toronto has had a headache." But now Toronto had turned over in bed and it was good.

Ken Pierson was with TDT for four years as administrative director. He left in 1991 because he felt it was the right time to go. He had created a framework in which both dream and organization could function productively and had a deficit reduction plan in place. But by moving the company onto the world stage, the additional costs would compromise that plan.

Creating the Works: Five

As artistic director, David continued to choreograph on a grand scale. *Sunrise*, like so much of David's work, draws upon painting and sculptures in a chain of arresting images danced in canon and in unison. David describes his motivation for the work:

> One day it occurred to me that the nineteenth century had just that moment died and, having fought with its images and values all my life, its sudden absence, like the death of a parent, created an instant nostalgia in me for the romance, heroism and pursuit of freedom that this period embodied. I turned to the German composers, and the painters Delacroix, Gericault, and Turner. Their storms and shipwrecks spoke to me of passion and adventure and breaking free from hollow forms that, no matter how beautiful, must be abandoned like shells on a seashore.

In appreciation of this work, David received the Clifford E. Lee Award and the Dora Mavor Moore Award for best new choreography in 1987. He believes that the achievements of the production were due in part to Ron Snippe's ability to capture the visual mood with his astonishing lighting designs.

Christopher continued his choreographic output with *Go Yet Turning Stay* in 1986 which received a Dora Mavor Moore Award and, in 1987, *Handel Variations* explored canon and motif work for a full company ensemble. *green evening clear and warm* was an exploration of dramatic ambiguity with its emphasis on conjuring arms and bodies tumbling in space. In 1988, he created *Artemis Madrigals* to Stravinsky's "Duo Concertant" for five dancers. When the

company took it to New York, Jack Anderson, praising House's creativity, noted a similarity to Balanchine's earlier work to the same music:

> Although Artemis was the Greek goddess of the hunt and the moon, no mythological story is told here. Nevertheless, as the dancers kept twisting around one another, they could have been simultaneously hunters and hunted. Both Balanchine's *Duo Concertant* and *Artemis Madrigals* end with a yearning duet, possibly because Stravinsky's melancholy finale invites choreographic introspection....

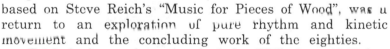

The emotional intensity and raw physicality of *Artemis Madrigals* signalled a new maturity in Christopher's choreography. He would then go on to create works such as *Noli Me Tangere* and *Island*. *Island*, based on Steve Reich's "Music for Pieces of Wood", was a return to an exploration of pure rhythm and kinetic movement and the concluding work of the eighties.

Trish had not choreographed for TDT since 1986 but as part of her contribution to dance, she wrote a very accessible book on choreography called *Form Without Formula*. Published in 1989, the book articulates her vision of the art of creating dances and it remains a valuable text for young dancers in post-secondary institutions.

Trish's nature works of the early eighties celebrated the sea and the sky. In 1990 she was creating again for TDT. *Gaia* was her first work which explored feminine spirituality through female archetypes and their relationship to the earth. *Gaia* marks the beginning of what she terms "healing dances" and would later be a part of *Dancing*

the Goddess, a project developed after Trish became an independent choreographer.

Shooting from the Hip

Succeeding in New York had been an unspoken dream of the founders, and Canadian audiences already excited by the new vitality of TDT, really sat up and paid attention when the New York critics acknowledged the Canadian company as "Heavy Artillery from Toronto." Toronto Dance Theatre's first visit to New York in 1985 was at a smaller but prestigious venue, Brooklyn College. In 1991, Ken Pierson arranged for them to perform at the historic Joyce Theater. It was a calculated risk that paid off, both at the box office and in print. The programme included James Kudelka's *15 Heterosexual Duets*, Trish's *First Music*, Christopher's *The Court of Lions*, and David's *Dreamsend*.

Dreamsend, subtitled "A melodrama in 12 moving pictures" and choreographed to the music of Anton Webern, explores the taboo of incest between a brother and sister which precluded its inclusion in the Sunday family matinée. Janice Berman, critic for *New York Newsday* was, for David, one of the few who had a real understanding of the work:

> Send the kiddies out of the room while we discuss *Dreamsend*, a piece about the wages of sexual repression ... with its replication of childhood traumas. [It] is about as horrifying and sophisticated as dance gets.... The brother and sister could be any couple whose love is forbidden, and the resultant emotional chaos,[is] delivered in a series of moving tableaux broken by blackout.... The grimness of figures confronting their worst nightmares is reminiscent of Paul Taylor's *Last Look*. Yet the sensuality of the draped nudes embracing before an audience of three children who

"witness love as an ideal," the stunning pantherine quality of Bill Coleman as an angel and the final agonized scene in which the angel, boy and girl (Coleman, House, and Braaf) pass down a row of black-veiled dancers carrying white flowers, mark Earle as yet another original voice. This is a company whose visit is most welcome.

This was not the only critical praise for the company. Anna Kisselgoff, in the *New York Times*, confidently stated, "the splendid works on view come out of a mainstream dance mentality, and if they are not experimental in an extreme sense, they are not what you see in New York. Go to them with big, bold dancing in mind." Kisselgoff endorsed the entire programme, but guest choreographer James Kudelka's *15 Heterosexual Duets* truly moved her. Kudelka's style, described as neoclassical, translates easily to the modern dance vocabulary and he had welcomed David's invitation and the challenge of working with the versatile TDT dancers. This abstract work of fifteen duets, danced to Beethoven's haunting *Kreutzer Sonata*, intricately and sculpturally interweaves the various partnerships. Kudelka's movement invention, kinetic and sensorial in nature, brings another level of appreciation to Beethoven's score. Graham McKelvie eloquently summarized his experience of learning the introductory duet with Laurence Lemieux:

15 was one of the most challenging pieces I've ever done. James would ask for what seemed impossible then calmly wait until we achieved it. The striking images we created, come from a beautifully dense exchange between two people. Often Laurence and I would be laughing as we lay on the floor, having fallen down when we had not achieved the precarious balance needed not only to give a thing its beauty but to make

it work at all. That is the significance of James' work, the beauty, structure, and architecture of his movement are one and the same.

15 Heterosexual Duets has been a unique contribution to TDT's repertoire ever since.

Lesser Value?

Public funding for any arts organization has always demanded financial and artistic accountability in return. As Canada entered the nineties and the provincial and federal governments were operating under severe fiscal restraints, so the grants to "arm's length" agencies diminished and the pressures for accountability increased. In June 1991, the board received a startling letter from the Canada Council which announced that the funding to TDT was to be reduced by $15,000. The main reason given for the reduction was not simply that the Dance Section itself was operating under severe budgetary restrictions but rather that the reduction was based "on artistic assessments received over the past couple of years" and "the financial health of the company." The Council's letter recognized the company's unique place within the national dance community, citing its longevity, popularity, international success, and dancers as factors for its success but ominously referred to the crisis of 1981:

> Today we are seeing those kinds of problems emerge again: the accumulated deficit is becoming more threatening, and many of our assessors are questioning the company's current artistic direction.... Our assessors have no problems with the production values of your company ... the problem lies in the programming. Our assessors generally agree on the remarkable talent of Christopher House and generally support the last work of David Earle. They also applaud the addition of James Kudelka's excellent work.... However, the other works created or remounted by the founders of the company are perceived to be of a lesser value towards the company's advancement and overall development of the art form.

The letter concludes by encouraging the board to focus on artistic merit and financial health, promising to "re-evaluate" and to continue to "monitor [TDT's] financial health."

This letter was a blow to David. It was Clifford Beatty, president of the board, who addressed the issues raised by the Council. He expressed shock at the assessors' remarks, pointing out that these concerns had not been raised in five years of correspondence. He listed the accomplishments of the company's 1990–91 season and cited the comments they had received in grant notifications over the past five years. In addition, he reminded the Council that the company had been awarded supplementary grants, totalling $105,000 for "artistic stature and demonstrated need" in 1989 and 1990. The restoration of the grant was not, however, the major issue. It was the implication that the work of Trish and Peter was of lesser value. Peter and Trish did not subscribe to the current demands of "style" or innovation. Their works had not been created for the market place, nor for the ease and accessibility of an audience and they trusted that audiences would understand the value of their artistic statement.

> My understanding of an artist is she is not after popularity, she is after making a real contribution to society. That is the difference between commercial and artistic ... you are encouraged by funding bodies themselves to learn marketing until you just about die. Of course you want people there, but at what price? ... it is things of the soul that matter.

David could not bring himself to tell Trish the reasons he was reluctant to programme her work. Trish remembers:

> I was torn in two because he [David] wasn't programming me. We didn't even speak for four months and we had been so close. Then he came back from a tour in Poland wearing a funny green shirt, and I saw him in the upstairs lounge and we just hugged. He said, 'Oh, they loved your work in Poland,' and we started talking again.

If the people in Poland understood the work, Trish could not comprehend why Canadians couldn't have the same opportunity. Her relationship with David was back on familiar ground but the concerns of the Canada Council made it difficult for him to support her artistry and the directions in which she was taking it.

Creating the Works: Six

In 1992, marking his choreographic return to TDT, Peter Randazzo completed his trilogy of works inspired by the paintings of Edward Hopper. *Summer Evening* was a large ensemble work with a complex set. Peter had noted the versatility and flexibility of dancer Sean Marye and sculpted the lead role on him with partner Suzette Sherman. Of the work, Robert Everett-Green said in *The Globe and Mail*:

> The piece came alive for me at the middle when Sean Marye broke from an enforced reverie for a brief writhing grasping solo; and at the end, when Marye and Suzette Sherman welded snippets of 1940s social dancing into a spiky, dangerously funny duet. Both episodes seemed to grapple after all the things unnamed and unpictured in Hopper's canvases, with their contained hysteria and mysterious simplicity.

Sadly, *Summer Evening* was Peter's last work for TDT. His contributions to the company remain as a remarkable and prolific body of choreographic invention and artistry and a major contribution to Canadian modern dance.

That same year, Trish announced that she would leave the company to work on her own. "David couldn't tell me [about the letter from the Canada Council]. He said to me 'you need to work in a different context here [TDT] other than death and the Goddesses.' By then we were older and it was harder and there were all these other forces...." In a candid interview with Paula Citron, Trish gives her reasons for leaving:

Bookers don't like me ... I'm not interested in choreographic forms because I am concerned with content and emphasis on content is an embarrassment. I believe in responsibility, that my work must have a positive influence on the world. Art needs spirituality to help human evolution, it needs wider perspectives.

Those "wider perspectives" and deeper roots had been explored in *Mandala*. It was a symbolic work honouring the life-force by celebrating the central mystery of the female body. The work is about transformation. *Mandala* employs the shared movement of ten women working in unison and in duets. The piece was longer (twenty-two minutes) than most of Trish's work because of its ceremonial nature. The repetition of theme reinforces the sense of ritual, the message of the power of the feminine, and the value of working in relationship. It was significant for Beatty that Rosemary James was five months pregnant when she danced in this piece. *Mandala* was Trish's final offering as a resident choreographer at TDT, although the company continues to remount her works. In his review of *Mandala*, William Littler wrote:

> Beatty being Beatty, it said more than it initially appeared to say, resonating from a centre of simple Grahamesque movement full of unisons, stretched limbs, and geometric patterning to speak of things deeply felt ... the dancers do not move as if kinetic activity were the purpose for the exercise.... For Beatty, as for Graham, movement isn't an end in itself: it is a way of visualizing our interior landscape.

Mandala was on the same program as David's new work, *Untitled Monument*. It, too, reflected an interior landscape — a darker view of the "new age" and perhaps, one that reflected his own difficulties in dealing with God and Mammon:

> A disturbing piece, ostensibly a monument to affluence gone askew, [it] uses contrasting features in the film music of Japan's Toru Takemitsu to underline the narrative of individuals lost in a system that, although it appears to be flourishing, is spiritually empty.

David continued to choreograph in spite the demands of his position as artistic director. He created *Angels and Victories* for the Polish Dance Theatre, performed both in Warsaw and at the Edinburgh Festival in 1992 and he also contributed a duet to *Romeos and Juliets* for Rhombus Media. This film received the Press Award from France's Grand Prix International de Video Dance de Sete, and a Gemini Award from the Canadian media.

Early Departures, Christopher's work to John Rea's dissonant music, "Kubla-Khan: Dirge-refrains," explores the issue of male conformity and social responsibility. In conversation with Francis Mason, he explains that *Early Departures* wasn't planned to be a piece about Aids. "I realized it was a piece about many people like me who are not HIV but who are asking, 'How do we help?'" Four male dancers, identically dressed like stock market traders: white shirts, dark pants, and red ties made up the cast. Michael Trent comments:

> I have a great affinity for *Early Departures*....
> I was brought in because Christopher was
> going to dance ... he asked me to stand in
> for him so he could watch the process from

the outside ... he was very generous and he gave me a couple of performances. My first performance unfortunately, was a little stressing. It was during a high school matinee ... it's difficult music, it's four guys ... and the kiss at the end didn't go over very well [with the students]. I was so disappointed and distraught afterwards.... I just felt that I had given so much to this piece and it meant so much.... In retrospect, I understand why they had that reaction.

The founders' choreography always remained consistent with their personal visions centred in universal truths, reflecting contemporary society through the lenses of spirituality, the visual arts and history. Christopher's work had to this point been quite formalistic and intellectual. His choreography now began to attach itself more directly to the emotional content surrounding current issues.

The Twenty-Fifth Anniversary

The five years under David's artistic directorship had been, despite all the difficulties, a time of great achievement which was celebrated during the twenty-fifth anniversary season in November of 1993. For the anniversary program, David stayed true to the works that he, the audiences, and performers had loved over the years. To represent himself he chose *Baroque Suite* and *Boat, River, Moon*. To exemplify the diverse quality of Peter's choreography, the company performed *Recital* and *Enter the Dawn* and David chose *Seastill* and *Skyling*, two of Trish's most eloquent and serene pieces, to represent her. Christopher's *Animated Shorts* and *Artemis Madrigals*, were remounted and he also created two new works, *Encarnado* and *Four Towers*. All the works appeared on two different programmes, featuring one work apiece from the founders and two works (one old, one new) from Christopher. "The idea — a good one," wrote Robert Everett-Green, "was to show both where the company had been and where it's going."

The anniversary programme afforded David the opportunity to express his feelings and thanks in print: "This language has been the principle strength of the company in its touring globally. It is the way the dancers move that has been a through line of the company's success

since it's inception." He is particularly poignant in his thanks to Suzette Sherman:

Suzette has been "the woman in my life" — my wife on tour, my daughter, my companion in every corner of Canada and around the world. Dancing with her ... Celebrates sixteen years of collaboration. Peggy Baker called her one of the undersung dancers of this company (and there are many in modern dance), and I have watched and been inspired by the evolution of this artist through her indomitable will and commitment to the art form that is without equal in my experience. Suzette and her husband, Glenn, are two precious friends who have certainly helped keep me on the earth.

The two-week season finished in style with a gala performance. Robert Everett-Green wrote:

David Earle stood on the stage of Premiere
Dance Theatre Wednesday evening, looking
and sounding for all the world like Rip Van
Winkle. Twenty-five years had gone by, and
honest, folks, he'd hardly noticed. Working
hard at something you love can do that to
you, more than sleeping ever could, even in
legend. And then one day somebody points to
calendar, and you realize that Toronto Dance
Theatre, which Earle founded with Patricia
Beatty and Peter Randazzo, is twenty-five
years old.

It seemed impossible for the company to receive a
better birthday present than a successful anniversary
home season but a paragraph in the Toronto anniversary
programme indicated that New York audiences had out-
done themselves and given TDT a most extravagant gift:

With over a month to go before Toronto
Dance Theatre opens at the Joyce Theater,
the run is almost completely sold out....
Another highlight of the season is that the
company will be performing at the Joyce on
its actual birthday. It was twenty five years
ago, on December 2nd, that the company first
performed at Toronto Workshop Productions.

The New York tour was a climax to the accumulated successes of Toronto Dance Theatre over the past twenty-five
years. The anniversary celebration also marked the beginning of an important time of transition for the company.

Next in Line
By 1993, David was exhausted by his responsibilities as artistic director. Planning seasons, ordering programmes, choosing choreographers, dancers, teachers, and
musicians, scheduling classes and workshops, and continuing his own choreographic process was demanding
enough. The lack of dialogue with Pierson and the emotional pulls he felt over not being able to support his fellow founders, placed a tremendous drain on his creative
energies. The incredible drive of Christopher House, his
long relationship with David as his mentor and with the
company, and his comfortable working relationship with
Ken Pierson made him the logical person to support

David in his task. In the spring of 1993, Christopher was named associate artistic director. Of his appointment, he says, "I think from the time Kenny [Pearl] left, I was actually a de facto associate artistic director. David and I worked very closely and we conferred on most artistic issues, planned tours together and I started to go to board meetings because David didn't like to go." By June 1, 1994, the transition was complete: David became artist in residence and Christopher took on the role of artistic director.

6

Christopher House, 1994–

Christopher House was born on May 30, 1955 in St. John's, Newfoundland. Together with his older sister Rosemary and his younger brother Peter, he had a comfortable childhood. Encouraged by their mother, all three children played the piano, although Christopher preferred to learn primarily by ear. His father was a successful neurologist, who would go on to become the lieutenant-governor of the province in 1997. His brother pursued a career in law, and his sister became a film-maker. Given his family's achievements, it is not surprising that Christopher would also be successful in his chosen field, becoming the artistic director of the largest modern dance company in Canada.

Growing up, Christopher knew that he did not fit in with the conservative social climate in St. John's.

Newfoundland at that time was very dark. St. John's was so isolated, with such a homogeneous culture and a very narrow view of "acceptable" male behaviour. It felt very limiting, so that early on I knew, even before I knew I was gay, that I needed to leave. I couldn't honestly fit in and become my own person.

"We trained him and encouraged him. It is only right that he should do things his own way."

Peter Randazzo, 1998

He excelled academically in high school and went to the University of Ottawa to study political science. Ultimately, Christopher envisioned a career as a diplomat in the foreign service, so he spent the summer of his third year in Montreal studying Chinese. When he returned to Ottawa for his final year of political science, he enrolled in a theatre course called movement for actors, taught by Elizabeth Langley. It was a course that would radically change the direction of his life. Christopher recalls: "Elizabeth's experience had been with the Graham technique, which she had rejected in the strongest terms and she worked mostly with improvisation. She was kind of 'anti-technique' at that time." Whatever Langley was doing, Christopher was hooked.

He finished his political science degree, taking almost exclusively theatre courses in his final year. In Christopher, Langley must have recognized a person with incredible potential for a professional dance career. Surprisingly, she cautioned Christopher about the difficulties of being a dancer. Disregarding her advice, Christopher left thoughts of his career in diplomacy behind and went in search of dance instruction.

He continued his training with Canadian dancer, Nikki Cole, who had taught a master class in dance in Ottawa. He says, "I found her very inspiring; she was very helpful to me. I went to visit her in New York over Christmas of 1976 and then decided I was moving to New York. I actually shared a loft with Nikki and with another Canadian dancer named Robin Collier for, I think, seven months." This experience provided the impetus to pursue dance as a full-time career.

Christopher, like many late starters, had an insatiable appetite and wanted to be immersed in many different styles but, interestingly, he did not take classes at the Graham studios. Hunger and honesty drove him back to Canada: "I was starving to death in New York. I wasn't that kind of resourceful person who could, you know, lie and get a fake social security card. I would always tell the truth and lose the job within a couple of hours, so it just wasn't going to happen." He chose to return to Toronto so that he could enroll in York University's Dance Program in 1977.

At York, where he was given advanced standing, he was able to concentrate on studio courses (ballet, modern, and composition) because he already had most of his academic requirements. At the same time, he was able to explore his interest in choreography. At the end of his first year, Grant Strate, chair of the Dance Department, organized the first National Choreographic Seminar. Robert Cohan, of the London Contemporary Dance Theatre, led the seminar as a guest choreographer, and many other notable professional choreographers and dancers, including Susan Macpherson, attended.

David Earle, who had seen Christopher in one of his classes in the spring of 1978, as well as in performance with 15 Dance Lab, recognized his talent. TDT needed extra dancers for their tenth anniversary performance series at the Royal Alexandra Theatre. David, through Susan Macpherson, invited Christopher to perform with the company and be part of the US fall tour. Although encouraged to remain with the company, Christopher knew he needed more training. He finished his degree in 1979 and rejoined TDT immediately after graduation, often assuming Peter Randazzo's roles in remounted works because of the similarities in their physiques and movement qualities.

Peter quickly saw Christopher's potential and talent as a choreographer and, after the opening of *Toss Quintet* (1980), Trish turned to the other founders and said, "I guess we are four." In response to the appointment as resident choreographer which followed his success, Christopher says, "I didn't feel I needed to be compensated because I felt the opportunity itself was pretty special. To be able to do it, [use great dancers, have studio time, commissioned music, costumes and lighting, and not to have to write grants,] was the best of both worlds."

By December 1982, Christopher had enough of a choreographic repertoire to fill an entire program at the Winchester Street Theatre. *Dances by Christopher House* included *Schola Cantorum, Toss Quintet, The Excitable Gift, Boulevard,* and *Fleet.* Although these pieces impressed the audiences, none of them would have the popularity of the works he created in the following years. Christopher's creative accomplishments in the eighties matched Peter's choreographic energy and output of the seventies.

In 1985, Christopher wrote a rather charming manifesto. It included the following statements and they provide a good picture of the man who would become the artistic director of Toronto Dance Theatre:

> I am a dancer and choreographer because I have an insatiable and ever-changing curiosity about movement and ideas, and because I feel that live theatre has a special significance in our time.
>
> I consider myself part of a rich tradition and consciously experiment with many aspects of twentieth century dance. I feel that a responsible artist achieves originality through synthesis, not self-conscious radicality or mindless rejection. I want to preserve all that remains alive and valuable.
>
> Music plays a major role in my work.... You should listen as you look to "see" my choreography....
>
> The humanistic energy shown by this community [TDT] makes a clear statement to the spectator. I want my dances to be life-affirming.

Christopher aimed to stay true to these goals. His efforts were rewarded when he won the Clifford E. Lee Award and the Dora Mavor Moore Award for his choreography in 1986 and the Dora again in 1989. During this period, he took short leaves of absence to dance with Les Grands Ballets Canadiens. There, he eagerly learned and performed Nijinska's *Les Noces*; danced the demanding dramatic principal role in Fokine's *Petrouchka*; performed his own solo *Schubert Dances*; and undertook the role of The Angel in James Kudelka's masterpiece, *In Paradisum*. These experiences fed his appetite for new and diverse artistic knowledge. He also learned much about the choreographic process and working with a larger company.

It was a meteoric rise. Christopher's talents as a dancer and choreographer were imperatives in that rapid advance but he owes much to David's mentorship, and to Kenny Pearl and Ken Pierson, with whom he established excellent working relationships. For the first time, TDT would have an artistic director for whom creative freedom and institutional accountability were not incompatible demands.

The New Partner

Christopher's appointment was made more difficult when Ken Pierson died suddenly in June 1994. Ken had been asked to rejoin TDT for the 1993 celebratory season and was on tour with the company in Frankfurt, Germany when he developed viral pneumonia. His death stunned the company and the dance world. The loss of Ken's advice, not to mention the administrative continuity, was a  terrible blow after all the celebrations. The board had to search for a new general manager during Christopher's first few weeks of becoming artistic director. It was a five week painstaking search. Jini Stolk, the executive director of the Toronto Theatre Alliance, emerged from the list of candidates as everyone's choice. She was to prove the ideal administrative partner for Christopher.

Ken Pierson's administrative acumen and respect for artistry helped to place Toronto Dance Theatre on the international stage, but the price for this reputation was expensive. At the time of his death, the accumulated deficit of the company was still almost as high as it had been when the building was purchased and renovated in the late seventies. It fell to Jini to control the crisis. She had to be strict when it came to production budgets and touring. New works had to be financially feasible and tours had to be within their means if the deficit was to be conquered. Jini also utilized her extensive experience to gain the company grants they had never applied for in the past. She further stabilized the company financially by clearly establishing the company's relationship with the Toronto Dance Foundation.

The Toronto Dance Foundation is the official owner of 80 Winchester Street. Since its purchase, the church had been the collateral for the company's line of credit with the banks. In 1995, the founders began utilizing the foundation as the financial basis for their independent productions. For example, the foundation helped to produce Trish's *Dancing the Goddess* series and video. Peter, Trish, and David hired Christine Forsythe, a former member of the TDT Board to administer the foundation for them. Christine, not being in the building, was not available to address the day-to-day needs and concerns of running the building and eventually, the foundation went into debt. Communication between the founders and Jini and Christopher was by now, tenuous at best.

Being the primary tenants, the bank asked Jini as general manager of TDT to manage the foundation. The bank generously gave TDT a line of credit based on their years of history with the bank, their reputation, and their potential grants. Since then, Jini has actively worked to assist all the tenants of 80 Winchester Street to maintain a prominent place in the dance community and in Cabbagetown itself. She has brought financial stability and clarity to the organization.

Jini stated that she could not have taken on the financial challenge TDT posed without Christopher's conviction and the ease with which he worked with the board. His diplomatic background served him well. He understood that the board "are volunteers, and not necessarily wealthy, and they work hard to help." With the controlled growth of the company in mind Kenny Pearl and Ellen Busby had cooperatively planned and Christopher had seen how Ken Pierson had managed to keep the institution relatively free of bureaucracy. He knew organizational structure had merits and understood that, as artistic director, he had an important role in developing and maintaining TDT as an institution. Jini recognized that TDT was beginning another era. With the approval of the board and Christopher, she hired a consulting company (Arts 4 Change) to help create a strategic plan for the future. As Christopher said:

> The value of an institution in the positive sense, is that it allows you to do what you want to do ... what we've tried to create is completely reflective of and adaptive to the

specifics of the artistic vision ... at any given time. If we decide it should be a fifteen week season with twenty-five people, if we only want to perform here or tour all over, or if we want to focus on live music, then you have the flexibility to do that because you are directly involved in the planning and that is the responsibility of the artist to make sure that everybody is aware of what you are thinking.... So Jini and I have very strong communication back and forth.

It is their comfortable working relationship and camaraderie that has enabled them to accomplish some pretty daunting tasks set them by the board. These, of course, were the same tasks that the founders had set for themselves in the beginning. Their six priorities continued, as always, to be: performing the work; reducing the deficit; touring the company internationally; creating goals and objectives for the long term future of the company; focusing on audience education and outreach; and establishing the building and the institution of TDT as a vital force within the community. Together Christopher and Jini are accomplishing these goals and keeping TDT on the edge of innovation.

"Time to Go"

In 1995, after nineteen years with the company, Suzette Sherman decided to leave, as did fourteen-year veteran Denis Joffre. For Suzette, it was a matter of loyalty to the founders' vision. For Denis, "from Christopher's perspective, he was going to need to have other visions [costume designers] come in with his work":

From my side, it was time for me to start working with other people ... the generation of dancers that I had come up with were spreading out and it presented itself as being the right time to go with that flow and reach out and stay with the momentum.

As early as 1993, when David was still artistic director, Trish and Peter were effectively no longer with the company. They attempted to work as independent artists with varied success. Trish always favoured using the

Winchester Street Theatre for her projects, but the sense of separation was very painful:

> It was like people smiled at us when we said something they didn't want to hear — as if they didn't hear us. There was no role for us after a while and that's why we reactivated the foundation and called it Regenesis. We kept ourselves alive for two years. Nobody else had any idea of what to do with us ... Peter was turned down because he filled out an application for a grant wrong. We have people down there [at council offices] who don't know who we are or what we did. It was very demeaning.

For David, the painful parting came later. In 1996, David, was honoured with the Order of Canada. It was also the year in which he would leave TDT to work on his own. His final statement that never appeared in the company's Newsletter for which it was written, gave his reason for leaving: "I believe it is time to take steps to preserve the values that are sacred to me in life and in dance, both in teaching and performance." David felt betrayed by the company he built. Christopher's plans for the company and the fact that the method of training was evolving in new directions, did not meet with David's approval. However, in retrospect, Peter says, "We can't complain about what Christopher is doing. We trained him, and encouraged him, it is only right he should do things his own way...." Trish comments on the difficulty of founder status: "It's not what happened, it's how it happened. It was secretive and deceptive. We are emotional and we felt like our lives were ripped apart. We were raw. Nobody meant to harm. The board didn't know what to do. None of us had a model for this difficult transition." The story is the same for a great many of Canada's artistic institutions.

Opening the Windows

The Winchester Street Theatre was a perfect venue for the presentation of works by the many independent choreographers in Toronto. Ron Snippe asserts that the theatre "is more than just a fancy rehearsal hall. We see it as a viable venue." Unfortunately, as with many buildings over a hundred years old, increased use led to increased repairs. By the beginning of the nineties, the poor condition of parts of the building meant that TDT had to stop renting out the theatre. Jini wanted the theatre restored to its former effectiveness as a theatre because of its historic associations, and she also needed it to provide a stable income for the foundation. The exterior of the building has been improved and restored, gardens planted, signs mounted, and the theatre painted. The lobby now includes a historical retrospective of TDT photographs and the whole building exudes a warm and welcoming atmosphere. The Winchester Street Theatre continues to serve independent choreographers and a number of festivals devoted to different kinds of performing arts, as well as providing space for many of the new TDT programs.

Most recently, Christopher has started the popular *Process Revealed* lecture series. Like the *At Home* series of the seventies, the *Process Revealed* attempts to demystify modern dance and make TDT more approachable for the general public and valued patrons. Christopher has also made student matinées and lecture demonstrations a priority, both in Toronto and on tour. He knows from years of experience at TDT that audiences don't just materialize, they have to be nurtured.

Most recently, Christopher has initiated the *Four at the Winch* series. This series is designed to be a forum for Canadian choreographers from TDT and elsewhere, to work with TDT's talented company dancers. This week-long season in the spring compliments the season at Premiere Dance Theatre in the Fall. The first *Four at the Winch* in March 1998, included choreographic works by Marie-Josée Chartier, Michael Trent, Mitch Kirsch, and Bill Coleman. Michael Trent describes the process:

> I've always been unable to tell what Christopher has really felt about my work. When Christopher asked me to do *Four at the Winch*, I was very surprised.... I invited him in at one point in the process and we began to talk for a few minutes.... We talked about certain issues [in my choreography], and I felt for the first time, he could ask me the right kind of questions and make me think about things. That was very satisfying for me.

Four at the Winch will become an annual event. Christopher and Jini have continued the founders' commitment to giving back to the community that has always been a part of the vision and of the mandate of TDT.

Creating the Works: Seven

Toronto Dance Theatre's recent history has not been all about restructuring and administrative strategy. Choreography continues to propel the company and since becoming artistic director, the majority of the new work has been Christopher's: *Apollo's Touch, Encarnado, Book of Hours, Pingo Slink* all met with critical acclaim. For *Apollo's Touch* Christopher collaborated with Arraymusic. This unique performance included musicians and dancers sharing the same stage. He remembers this work with particular fondness.

Two works that demonstrate Christopher's versatility as a choreographer are *Barnyard* and *Cryptoversa*. *Barnyard*, originally choreographed in 1993 and remounted in 1997, explores the nature of relationships with the full company; it is satiric, witty, and, at the same time, deeply compelling. *Cryptoversa* is in many ways the antithesis to *Barnyard*. Laurence Lemieux, "using her legs like compass points ... pricks through right angles and then melts into the floor. With

extensions like taffy pulls, Lemieux's languorous grace makes for some serious goosebump material." Lemieux, so technically adept and yet so dramatic, was the perfect muse for this difficult piece and received a Dora Mavor Moore Award for her performance, in May 1998.

During the 1997 Fall season, Christopher collaborated with Korean visual artist Kim Soo-ja on the work *Bottari*. In the same season, he invited the internationally renowned Indian choreographer, Chandralehka, to create *Namaskar*. Both works demonstrated the versatility of the dancers and Christopher's openness to the exploration of new themes and cultures.

Since Christopher's appointment as artistic director, besides maintaining the Canadian touring circuits, the company has toured to China and Japan, Europe, the USA, and India. Of the Japanese tour, Naoko Murakoshi, who was desperate to let the Japanese audience know about the Toronto Dance Theatre "because my experience of them had been so incredible," remembers:

> [At first] the audience response was mysterious. Their enjoyment of our work was harder to read than some of our audiences in Europe and North America. The last day when we concluded *Handel Variations*, we heard a wonderful "Bravo!" I bowed with thanks from the bottom of my heart. I found out later that this person was the publisher of *Dance Magazine* in Japan. His review of the company was highly complimentary.

On both trips to the Far East, TDT proudly represented Canada at official state functions. Again, the founders' vision, first dreamed of in 1968, of a company that would have international impact, continues to be realized.

Return to the Heartland

Of the founders at the time of writing, Trish is the only one who maintains a relationship and a presence in the building:

> It is a church. My family helped build this. I feel the history of it. Now there is a lot of change going on and I am trying to keep connected. It's delicate but I feel I am respected.

After leaving TDT Trish, working with other independent choreographers, presented *Dancing the Goddess*. The concept of the program was to link sacred ceremony with modern dance to celebrate the goddess archetypes. Dancer and choreographer Terrill Maguire explains:

> *Dancing the Goddess* was conceived as a total ceremonial event in which people would come to witness and be a part of the healing transformation process. It came from a feeling that there is a great need for the sacred function of art in our society. There is a lack of the sacred which connects to healing. What Trish did was put together works of people that had a healing intention. She had to do this apart from TDT. Many of her earlier works at TDT grew from a psychological focus; she had evolved and moved on to the spiritual as a place of reference in her work.... She made me believe it was possible to create something this huge.

Michael Trent was one of the choreographers invited to create for the second production:

> Suzette [Sherman] is somebody who is extremely important to me. She was very welcoming, generous and kind throughout my entire time at TDT. She took this guy who thought he knew everything and spent personal time coaching me on the Graham forms. I did a duet for Suzette as a homage to her. Trish asked us to do that as part of the second *Goddess* project.

Dancing the Goddess was the culmination of five years of intensive creative thought and work and, for Trish, the door to a more personal and sacred approach to art and life. Recognizing and respecting Trish for her passionate commitment to Canadian modern dance, Christopher will be presenting *Against Sleep* as part of the thirtieth anniversary season.

Peter's extraordinary body of work continues to be as exciting to watch today as it was when it was first presented to audiences. *A Simple Melody* was mounted by the Danny Grossman Dance Company in the winter of 1998. William Littler congratulated the company on reviving "such a distinctive page of our choreographic past. It is a service to Canadian dance." In the spring of the same year, Peter created a piece specifically in the style of a forties Graham work, for a young dancer who wanted to experience the Graham technique. The work revealed the depth of his knowledge and his ability to use the technique. Says Peter:

> David, Trish, and I are survivors and you cannot suppress survivors. You also cannot suppress the truth. Anything that is based in the truth will survive and, as you know, the truth will set us all free. I used to believe that I could only create through a negative ... now I can see that, at one time, I felt I had to be dying in order to be creative. Now, I feel very different. Relaxed and confident.

Since leaving TDT, David has founded his own dance company, Dance Theatre David Earle, in order to continue his own evolving choreographic vision. He has functioned as artist in residence at the Canadian Children's Dance Theatre and is in much demand as a guest artist, nationally and internationally.

In the spring of 1998, Kenny Pearl who is still associated with Toronto Dance Theatre, was asked to recommend a male dancer who could take on the role of the husband in *Appalachian Spring* with the Martha Graham Dance Company in New York. Kenny suggested Bill Coleman. David was invited to watch him rehearse in the studio on Winchester Street. It was the place where David had spent most of his creative life:

> Bill had come to Canada from England hoping to find in his own choreography, as he called it, "the heartland." Here was this young man, dancing the role of someone looking to the future. He was dancing his own narrative ... it brought tears to my eyes. To think that here was a dancer that I had trained and worked with, going off to dance this great role with my mentor's company. It was if it had all come full circle.

All circles in the creative process are ascending spirals and Toronto Dance Theatre continues to draw its inspiration from the wellsprings of the founders' vision, its strengths from the unreserved commitment of its dancers and support staff, and its future from its belief in the power of dance as a "life affirming" expression of those things that cannot be described in words and that lie "in the heart of myself."

7 THERE ARE TWO things that lie at the heart of Toronto Dance Theatre: the underlying spirituality embodied in the Graham technique and the theatrical ethic that sprang from this teaching. Dancers speak through their bodies, choreographers through their dancers, and musicians through their instruments. Given a different medium for expression, they can be as eloquent. These voices echo the reflections of the many who have been a part of the journey.

On Teaching

Trish: At the beginning none of us knew whether we were teachers. We didn't have that much experience, but we knew it was necessary to train the company. We had knowledge of the technique and knowing I could be a carrier of this great technique is what inspired me and got me through. It was a thrill and a challenge to show it to people who had never seen it. David taught the danciest classes; Peter taught challenging and exciting classes; you had to be brave and willing to risk, to really experience his value as a teacher. I feel I was the teacher who taught about weight, falling, and inner possession; I really analyzed it. My experience with the Alexander (Mitzvah) technique has

"Dance can suggest a whole life process...."

Christopher House, 1994

allowed me to prevent injury without losing emotional or physical intensity. The opening of the chest of the dancers changed the look of the dancers, it was emotionally freeing. It is a beautiful look; with the heart open, the spirit is free.

Susan Macpherson: Right from my first year with Toronto Dance Theatre I taught at the school, which was created to train dancers for the company. At first I was intimidated, but David was very encouraging. He said, "You've been to New York, so give the people here some of what you have learned. Don't compare yourself to the great teachers you've had. You have something to offer as well."

David: Graham's technique was in the process of evolution all through her life. In keeping with the spirit of her genius, it was not arrested at any point in time. Students of mine who return from sessions at the Graham School in New York are assured that I am not teaching "the Graham technique." I realize that, other than the floor work, which I tend to run without interruption, the largest part of the class are exercises and forms of my own invention. I teach Graham principles.

I think that the Graham principles are bigger than dance. They are about the recovery of instinct. It [class] is a big deal, it's important, I did this class the day my mother died; I did this class the day my father died. I believe it is a way of coming to terms with existence.

Peggy Baker: After the first few years of my training, I was sometimes allowed to take company class, and a lot of my learning was simply a function of being surrounded by great dancers. It was thrilling and terrifying to take class alongside my teachers: Susan

Macpherson, Barry Smith, Amelia Itcush, Keith Urban, Helen Jones, Merle Salsberg, Norrey Drummond, David Wood, Kathy Wildberger, and Kathryn Brown. Jackie Burroughs was often in those classes and Donald Himes. The most senior students were Mary Newberry, Pat Miner, Colleen May, Sam Chaitin, Larry McKinnon, Peggy Florin, and sometimes even musician, Ricardo Abreut, joined us. Company class was always taught by one of the three directors and the other two took class themselves.

Suzette Sherman: Teaching is learning. I talk about becoming the dancer I am, the person I am, as a result of having been at Toronto Dance Theatre. A huge chunk of that is the fact that teaching was so much a part of the experience of the people there. When I got there, everyone just did it. Teaching clarifies and makes for more perspective. When people say "maybe one day I'll teach, but right now I just want to concentrate on my dancing," all I can think is that you would have to dance half the length of time that you're going to have to dance if you taught like two classes. Teaching is the way you learn, that's the curious thing, it's a door that once you open ... you will find that it [the material] is more yours than it ever was. You learn more yourself as you pass it on, you are in more possession of it and it's just an amazing experience.

Michael Trent: Suzette was one of the people who saw that I had some teaching skills and some passion for that, based on how I approached the dancers [as a chore-ographer] and how I explained what I wanted — how I worked in that environment. She thought, "Here's some-one who needs to be a teacher, needs to explore that." It was through her that I made it into the School of the Toronto Dance Theatre and taught there.

Peter: I stopped teaching once in the eighties. I was teaching this class and not getting anything from the students. I stopped the class and asked, "Who here wants to be a great dancer?" No one put up their hand. I said, "Let me ask this again, 'Who here wants to be a great dancer, put up your hand.' No one put up their hand. I left the room and said to Billyann, 'I can't teach these students.' "

Trish: I have always taught composition and the creative work. Once in the early stages of the professional program, we showed a student choreographic workshop. Grant Strate came to watch and later wrote a letter to us saying that these "well-meaning students needed to study composition." I said to Danny [Grossman], "I'd like to do that but I have such a strong bias, I don't know if I can." He said, "Listen, you have a good bias; let them deal with it." That's how we started [composition classes]. Its called the choreographic process and it's wonderful.

Michael: My strongest connection with Trish is as a teacher. The way she prepared you with the material and her approach to the material was so integrated. There were all these large ideas that she would talk about: being present in the space and very centred, and working deeply and into the ground. I could actually feel them by the time class was over and I loved doing her classes. She is a phenomenal coach; she has a wonderful eye and one of her strongest skills is how she can work with a piece and how she can coach it and take it to another level.... Trish and I over the years have developed a friendship and she has grown to respect me as a teacher.... She is a wonderful lady, full of very specific ideas which, at times, [made] people roll their eyes and go, "Oh, Trish!" But many years later I think back to some of the things she told me when I was much less experienced, and I now think I understand what she was talking about.

Karen duPlessis: Trish taught me grounding, I would say for all her work, if you didn't really have an understanding on a deep level of your Graham technique, you would hurt yourself. If you didn't have it — that is, something that was part of the rehearsal process — she would show that. Every single dancer that I have ever seen who has gone through that process with her has come out of it with a different understanding of certain elements of dancing.... The other thing I learned about is that in the dance world, forgiveness is needed. The person I learned that from is Patricia; I have seen her forgive and forgive and forgive again.

Michael: [Peter] was a very interesting and dynamic teacher. People either loved or hated his classes. I liked them. I thought they were really quirky but there was something about his physicality that I found very interesting and very hard technically. I got a lot out of his classes.

David's classes are well-known across the country as being extremely popular. They are rooted in a really strong point of view; they are very physical and you really feel at the end of one of his classes that you experienced something.

Kenny Pearl: I'd finished my BA in English literature and was in New York at the Graham School. David, Pete, and Trish would ask, "When are you going to teach?" It was a huge opportunity, to only be at the intermediate level and come and do that.

Trish: Suzette was the real support for teaching, so were Rosemary James and Kim Piul. Billyann Balay, who ran the school for so many years, maintained the integrity of the training. She knew us really well and, as creative artists, we were a handful. She was fabulous with all three of us. She steered the ship through some dangerous waters. We are indebted to her.

Billyann Balay: As a teacher and then as principal of the school, I understood that dance — and our work in particular — was a profound physical, emotional, and intellectual experience. When I think about all the exceptional young people who came through the school in the 1980s, I remember with love and pride not only those who went on to dance with TDT and so many other companies across Canada, but also those who chose other directions in their lives. I know that their time at TDT was life-transforming, because it was for me. This is TDT"s most extraordinary legacy.

On Choreography

David: The first phase is like turning the handle on a faucet and inspiration comes gushing out. The Gods are speaking through you. You are following your intuition with deep reverence and conviction. You are always looking for truths in the human condition. What matters is that you pay attention to what is going on around you, as you are mining the source and creating. If you are paying attention and interested in other art forms you will be ready for the second phase when the Gods step out. In the second phase, you are left with the challenge of a craftsperson. You work your craft. You then create a body of work and establish a reputation. The final phase is, hopefully, a combination of those two phases. You regain some connection to your original source; you know how to fashion it and to work with consciousness to give it meaning.

Luc Tremblay: The *Miserere* was the ending part of a piece [*Exit, Nightfall*] which was bringing us through a long journey: falling from the sky to the earth, going through the inferno. We had to really feel each other as the whole dance was performed connected to one another in groups of five, exchanging our weight, lifting one another ... all this to a very peaceful score. You had the sensation of reaching illumination and, at the end, to symbolize this, we formed a three-level pyramid of human bodies. Performing this piece was certainly a highlight for me in my years with TDT.

Michael: I was as nervous as all get-out because Peter gives out the most difficult material. I remember being hugely challenged by the physicality of it. Just getting a chance to work with Peter was wild. He'd just throw out material and you threw yourself into it and just did it as best you could. He would coach you to make it happen.

Peggy: Peter was really into the physical extremes of the training: the really sharp, quick, percussive, jagged edges. A lot of times his dances were just a big visceral outpouring of physicality, really muscular, but based somehow in a sort of sexual energy — we were really aware of people being men and women — it was not an androgynous thing with him. He'd just sort of spew; pour out these big intricate chains of movement with lots of really clean changes of direction and bang! bang! up and down off the floor.

Michael: Christopher would start off in silence and for a week or two he'd just generate material. He tries to find a vocabulary, a set of physical combinations that speak; meanwhile he's doing lots of thinking on his own. The specific idea he's been inspired by — a series of photographs, paintings, or literature — he doesn't share that with us.

Peggy: David, of course, was sort of poet philosopher — painterly, almost a totally different kind of atmosphere in his classes and his work. There were lots of people in his dances, they were on a grand scale.

Peter: David is the only choreographer in the world who is a film-maker when he's trying to get to the image. Most choreographers are interested in movement, but David uses movement to get to the pictures of what he's looking at. It's a very unusual process. He never gets stuck in the movement; he cuts through that.

Karen: I always felt that I was travelling with David on his journey to choreography; I was in the passenger seat as opposed to being the back seat, wondering where you are going.... As a person, he's charismatic, forgiving, understanding, and accepting.

Suzette: I learned the *Baroque Duet* as an apprentice and danced it on a fairly regular basis all through my years at TDT. One of the dilemmas in modern dance is that often pieces are created for a certain event and then it's over and you never see it again. Ballet dancers get the opportunity to revisit roles ... now having been through the process, I can say, you're not even doing the piece when you first do it. There are just layers and layers that you learn about the piece and about yourself. It's a long way into the process before you are really able to start thinking about the piece and how glorious the music is ... to be able to ask yourself what does David mean about it being a love duet, when at first, on the surface, it just seemed like a beautiful abstract movement piece to glorious music.

Luc: My most vivid recollection of playing a superhero in Peter's *A Simple Melody*, was when we performed it in Niagara-on-the-Lake. During the piece, there's a section where we have a mock battle. The dancer I was fighting with actually hit me by accident on stage, and broke my thumb. In the final tableau, I was standing on

143

my shoulders and had to lift that same dancer.... I guess he won the battle. Such is the life of a superhero!

Karen: Peter has this amazing ability to draw people to him. I had the opportunity to rehearse the tango [from *L'Assassin Menace*] with Peter and that was great! He has no problem looking so deeply in your eyes, and despite anything he was going through at the time, that piercing, searching, beckoning quality was there. Peter's work always had that kind of intensity.

When I got married, I asked Peter if we could do tango at our wedding. We planned this as a big surprise. We learned the tango at home and Peter rehearsed us and at the end he added one of those Valentino poses ... going for my neck. He sent us off with his blessing. At the wedding, we disappeared to change. My sister, who was the only one who knew we were going to do this, asked everybody to sit down; the music came on, and we entered. Nobody knew it was us and you couldn't see our faces because of the hats we were wearing. When they realized it was us, nobody knew what to do. I thought they'd clap and think, "Oh, so cute," but when we stood to bow, everybody was crying; there wasn't a dry eye in the place. My sister said "I couldn't watch; it was too intense." That kind of typifies the impact of Peter's work onstage.

Michael: As a choreographer at TDT, I've really been allowed to take risks and grow.

Ron Snippe: Artistically, I like the idea of single night performances on tour. Often I'd create my own balance. If one piece had blue and all the others were blue, I'd adapt the designs to suit the programme. Sometimes I had to adapt and sometimes the conditions wouldn't allow us to adapt. For example, *Sunrise* has a very thin foil where lights are bounced on to the cyclorama. It was beautiful and muted. The foil was effected by any wave of movement. On tour in Germany, they turned on the air-conditioning system, which created quite a breeze. Suddenly, there were violent slashes of colour, like a horrible acid dream from the sixties. We couldn't turn the air-conditioning off, and we couldn't get to the cues fast enough. We'd get to a restful blue, then on the next cue they'd come roaring back and I'd go, "argh."

Karen: What I like about Christopher's use of music is the way he uses his imagination with it. The way he structures movement to music in my mind is very different. Some of it is choice of music but often the music is being composed while he is in the choreographic process. He never does what I would do. He never explains what he is doing. So once you see a piece completed you make of it what you will and it's so much more mysterious.

Christopher: The dancers inspire me, but I mostly tell them what to do. We don't choreograph by committee.

On Critics

Peggy: Critics are supposed to be bridge builders. People who are writing about dance should be investigating the artists they are writing about; they should be coming to watch class, rehearsal, not waiting for the press release to come out, not to sit in judgement, but to learn what's going on with the artists.

Trish: In dance criticism, it's much easier to talk about dances that are out of balance, dances with an excess of form or of feeling ... what you will be reading about when you read the critics is the writer's life as it is revealed by watching your dance.... It is not your feelings or your ego that is involved in a discussion of your dance. It is your work alone that is of interest.

Peter   Thank you William Littler; after a thirty-year career, you've reduced me to a "Looney Tune."

On Dancing

Peggy: Our bodies hold the histories of our dancing in them. Nobody is making up things that were not born in their own body.... By virtue of being an individual, if I go into the core of myself to make something, it is going to be unique, not because I made up the steps, but because I am myself. That's what is very beautiful about those three [the founders]; they still use the Graham technique but have taken it in very different directions ... to use as a basis for their own creative lives.

Trish: The dancers who brought all this choreography through the years were sumptuous and special, full of character and presence. They were the bright lights that carried so much of the repertoire and brought the dances to life. Their dancing and presence is treasured.

Michael: The largest chunk of my professional career has been at Toronto Dance Theatre. You can't help but be influenced simply by the longevity of that relationship. I feel what has been phenomenally important to me is the people I have worked with — phenomenal creators — and to be able to present that work in all kinds of venues around the world.

Coralee McLaren: I feel so honoured to have danced at a time where I experienced all four of them [the founders and Christopher]. I have grown up here.

Grace Miyagawa: When I'm dancing Trish's works, I see movement as sculpture, because Trish uses the body as a piece of art. I love the stillness and simplicity of her movement. Being still on stage is the most difficult aspect of performing, because it makes a dancer feel vulnerable. From working with Trish, I have learned that stillness in the body can direct energy and have a powerful impact on the audience.

Christopher: TDT has always been blessed with wonderful dancers. The company's history overflows with images of passion, imagination, technical derring-do, musical audacity, brilliant performances imbued with tremendous belief in the act of dancing — and the potential of dance to enrich our lives.

Peter Randazzo, Patricia Beatty, and David Earle set the example and, in the process, created a phenomenal breeding ground for dancers.

The succeeding generations at TDT reveal a "who's who" of Canadian (and often international) dance ... the list is mind boggling and goes on and on.

On Ricardo Abreut, the "Silent Partner"

Billyann: Ricardo Abreut had a deep, lifelong devotion to the training of dancers and musicians. He was an artistic and spiritual mentor to generations of students at the school. He even (unbelievably to those who knew and loved him) ran the school for a year. Ricky conceived and directed two national accompanists' symposia which not only influenced the careers of many musicians involved in dance but also raised the stature of accompanists to equals with teachers in the training process....

He was playing for class the day before he died on July 12, 1995.

Trish: He kept the crew and the dancers going and together. He was very committed to us; he was the silent fourth founder of TDT. He was the caretaker of the soul ... he was the person who kept everyone together. He influenced generations of dance students.

Peggy: The people who were playing for classes were amazing musicians and people would come and sit in because they wanted to learn. Like Ahmed, who learned everything from Ricardo, and later people were coming to hear Ahmed, and now people are coming to hear people who were coming to hear him! It's a big cycle of sharing.

Ahmed Hassan: In 1979, I was playing drums in Ottawa for Le Groupe de la Place Royale. Ricardo phoned me and offered me a job playing at TDT. I gave up my job, my apartment, and was in Toronto in two weeks. When I arrived, no one knew anything about it! I wrote a letter to the board and, before I knew it, I had a contract.... I think it was the first written contract they had ever offered!

Peggy: Ricardo sat like royalty at those drums, the master of his domain. It was really quite imperial.

On the Music

Ahmed: The Graham technique classes were a very good way to grow as a musician — to be able to sculpt and to refine what you were doing so that, when you were working with the dancers, it was just — Ah! Magic!

Ann Southam: I was just starting to work with electroacoustic music [music directly on tape]. This particular sound works well with dance ... it is pure sound and pure energy. If you visualize anything, you visualize the sound itself. It is a physical presence, along with the dancers.

I had to rent the sound system and humph it to the theatre, set it up, and run it myself — which I loved! To have my music played in a theatre for the public over a big sound system was quite exciting.

With Peter, it was like there was always a thin thread of barbed wire running through the music.... I did most of collaborations with him. Two of my favourite pieces I did for Trish: *Seastill* and one of my earliest pieces, and *Against Sleep*, which remains a dance I absolutely love because of the ambiguity of it. Maybe not for Trish, but for me, it could mean all kinds of things.

The founders encouraged Canadian composers.... Trish was looking for Canadian composers way back in 1966. I

composed *Momentum* for her and have been working with them all ever since. They would give me a framework to work with and I would go away and bring the sound to their narrative. With Peter and *Encounter*, we worked independently. When we put it together it worked marvellously well. I was thrilled with what Christopher did with *Glass Houses*. I am very happy to be a part of any of these dances.

Peggy: Just look at some of the people who arrange music for dance. Most of those composers literally are partners with someone in the dance world: John Oswald and Holly Small; Eric Kandinsky and Katherine Duncanson; me and Ahmed; and before I was with Ahmed, I was with Michael Baker and now he's with Marie Josée Chartier; Henry Kucharzyk and Susan Cash, these musicians were coming in to play for class. They were making music for their girlfriends who were making dances and they were learning how to create music a lot through the dance world.

On Collaborating

Kenny Pearl: I felt really blessed in so many ways during my years at TDT. The blessings all come from the people involved. I always felt such dedication and commitment, talent, and intelligence. The great steps taken by TDT ... were always the result of the people coming together, of so many generous and deeply talented people.

Denis Joffre: I got my education at TDT. I knew nothing or very little. I just followed these people along and they took me for a ride. One of those rare treats is that you can have a body of your work emerge with someone else's work. David really represented the romantic emotion ... a striking flow of humanity on stage. With Trish, I got to explore areas I could never imagine ... to work with Graham Coughtry, for example.... She is a keen observer of classic beauty and of the depths of a deeper beauty. Peter always respected me as an artist. He once said of a set I had painted, "This is great! It's a work of art." There was a respect there, even though we're sort of on two different planets; it was one of the times we really connected.

Ron: I learned lighting at Brock University under Don Acastor who was also TDT's first lighting designer. Don talked about dealing with artistic temperament. They, the choreographers, talk about their work and we have to interpret for them. Trish hated strong colour; she didn't want them to be brassy. David was much more inspired by imagery. He described paintings and films to inspire or motivate me. Peter was pretty much black and white. He had an idea about what he wanted, or he left it up to me and commented as I was doing it on the fly. Christopher has strong ideas but he gives me a great deal of freedom. Christopher can be concerned with lighting important facial features or where the choreography is sculptural, but he prefers general lighting where all the details can be seen.

Christopher: K.C. [Coombs], Penny [Olorenshaw], Aisling [Sampson], and Lori [McLean] kept their spirits up — and our spirits as well — through many near disasters, the details of which are stranger than fiction. These intrepid women would not give in. The success of the tour [to India] was largely due to their efforts.

Trish: Ron Snippe has been with TDT for the better part of twenty-five years. He has lit over a hundred of the repertory works which means collaborating closely with all the choreographers. He has toured internationally, often managing the dancers and the crew as far afield as Western Europe and South America. He has been there with real support for complicated or especially courageous and risky seasons and productions. He is now working with architects to redesign Winchester Street Theatre. Ron is certainly one of the mainstays of this company ... a serious player in this piece of Canadian dance history.

Ron: My artistic side enjoys lighting design but its very difficult to do full time. I often wear other hats. First I was their lighting guy and technical director, then lighting guy and stage manager on tour. By 1989 I was lighting guy and company manager and booking tours, then I imploded and fled to Mexico.

Ann: I collaborated with David on *Boat, River, Moon* which was David's interpretation based on the Noh genre.... I'm thinking, "what do I know about Japanese music? which is, nothing!" ... I remember thinking it was a raw and haunting sound. I plowed ahead in spite of my ignorance. It seemed to be fine with David. I think I proceeded with a *felt* sense rather than a conscious, intentional approach.

I listen to everything they say, watching their body language, facial expressions, their way of speaking, to get a sense of what it was they were trying to convey. I don't remember what the people say, it's the experience of being with their energy. I was picking up different stuff....

Trish: David would always say I was so hard on my collaborators, "But David," I'd say, "so many of them became my friends...."

Christopher: With Karen [duPlessis] I would do something and she would read it in a way that wasn't exactly what I had done, but it was exactly right in terms of intention, phrasing, fitting into the style of the piece. In fact, she would influence how the piece would develop and that is the best kind of collaboration.

Ann: Working at TDT had an enormous effect of my life and career.... I adored the movement and drama of it all.... I loved everything: the people I worked with, the dancers, the dances, the theatre. It was a very, very inspiring and nourishing time for me.

On Mentoring

Suzette: I was David's assistant and I sometimes used to think to myself, "I can't believe you're saying that to David Earle!" ... but I did. The standing joke was that for every good idea I would get a quarter and I swear he owes me millions ... he probably has a different tally! It is so thrilling to me when he uses something I've said.

Peter: Over the years, David has always stood by me, through all my crackups and my love affairs and my ups and downs, and that in itself says a lot about the man.

Suzette: Trish was a huge and powerful example. She taught me a lot about community. The biggest thing was to see a woman who ... was just larger than life, teaching, choreographing — in every context. She has dignity and power and magic. She wasn't afraid of being extraordinary, so there was a whole possibility to be explored [for me, as a young woman]. I became aware that she really embodied female qualities that I had not been exposed to. She continues to inspire and blaze trails. She's not afraid of being strong.

Terrill Maguire: Trish helped me understand I had something to give that was important, valuable, and worth the effort. She made the impossible, possible. I think that's something we do for each other. We give back perspective when either one of us has misplaced our task. The task is about the healing sacredness of art.

Ron: In my mind, the impact of the company and the school is huge. I think a lot of people have a different level of appreciation of the importance this organization has had on their lives.... Partially this is why I've stayed; there is always something interesting going on. This has been my longest professional relationship, although I've always worked within the dance community at large. My other ongoing relationships within the dance community include Danny [Grossman], Robert [Desrosiers], and independent choreographers.

Ann: There was tremendous support of me. They were willing to try anything I brought them. It was like Heaven!

Last Words

David: Do you have to audition as an artist for a lifetime? Isn't there some cut-off point where you say, "like it or lump it." If no one will lay a foundation, we can't hope for something new.

Donald Himes: You ask me how I see them? Trish: Passionate; Peter: Possessed; And David? Profound.

Christopher: It is well-known that the hothouse life of a dance company is tremendously complex, filled with twists and turns, snakes and ladders, heartaches, thrills, triumphs. Risk is essential, both creatively and personally. With nothing ventured, nothing is gained.

The Dancers . . .

The following is a list of company dancers taken from the computer archives at Toronto Dance Theatre. It does not include all of the over four hundred people who appeared with TDT in *Court of Miracles*. David Earle and Trish Beatty were consulted. The alphabetical list includes apprentices and guest artists who appeared or toured with the company.

Abbott, Darren
Abreut, Ricardo (musician, dancer,
    guest choreographer)
Adams, Lawrence (guest)
Alton, Kate
Andersen, Kirstin

Baker, Peggy (apprentice, guest)
Balay, Billyann
Barclay, Lara
Beatty, Patricia
Beckon, Stephen
Blewchamp, Anna
Bobrow, Eric
Boissonot, Lucie
Bonin, Darren
Bouchard, Sylvie
Braaf, Miriane
Brown, Kathryn
Burr, Monica
Burroughs, Jackie (guest)

Chaiton, Sam
Chase, Sarah
Chiles, Wendy
Coleman, Bill
Conway, Michael

Desroisiers, Pascal
Desroisiers, Robert
Douglas, Bill
Drummond, Norrey
Dubois, Marie-Josée
duPlessis, Karen
Durling, Todd

Earle, David
Elias, William

The Dancers and the Dances

"Sumptuous and Special"

Trish Beatty, 1998

Ferguson, Nancy
Fisher-Credo, Cornelius
   (apprentice)
Flanders, Charles (Chuck)
Franca, Celia (guest)

Gardiner, Terry
George, Monica
Goodwin, Gary
Grider, Christopher T.
Grossman, Danny

Hendin, Judith
Highway, Dennis (René)
Himes, Donald
Hochoy, David (guest)
Holloman, Merle
Hood, Susanna
Hoskins, Daryl
House, Christopher

Irving, Kevin
Itcush, Amelia
Ivanochko, Sasha

Jackson, Graham
   (guest poet)
James, Rosemary
Jones, Helen
Jones, Rosemary

Kirsch, Mitch
Kudelka, James (guest)

Lachambre, Benoit
Ladd, Ron
Landerman, Suzanne (guest)
Lanier, Sherry
Leigh, Angela (guest)
Leigh, Nenagh (guest)
Lemieux, Laurence
Lidge, Dindi
Littleford, Julian

Macpherson Susan
Maguire, Terrill (guest)
Mann, Marc
Marcus, Howard (guest)
Marye, (Michael) Sean
McGarrigle, Kevin
McKelvie, Graham
McLaren, Coralee
McNicolls, Learie

McPhail, Robin
Messer, Jan
Miller, Judith
Miner, Pat
Miyagawa, Grace
Moore, Claudia
Moore, Miguel (Michael)
Morin, Jean-Louis
Murakoshi, Naoko
Murillo, Steven

Parks, Greg
Pettitt, Sara
Presseault, David
Preston, John
Pritchard, Kathleen

Quaintance, Michael

Randazzo, Peter
Redhead, Crispin
Robertson, James
Roope, Clover (guest)

Salsberg, Merle (Germaine)
Sasso, Julia (guest)
Small, Almond
Small, Holly (guest)
Smith, Barry (Artis)
Smith, Lois (guest)
Sparling, Peter (guest)
Stefan, Sonya
Stewart, Ron

Teillet, Jeannie
Tennant, Veronica (guest)
Thompson, Clive (guest)
Tremblay, Luc
Trent, Michael
Trentham, Gerry (guest)

Urban, Keith
Urban, Susan

Wallin, Cristal
   (guest teacher)
Walsh, Seth
West, Laura
Wildberger, Kathy
Wolofsky, Carly (guest)
Wood, David
Woodland, Dale
Woods, Carolyn (guest)

The Dances . . .

This list includes all of the choreography performed by Toronto Dance Theatre from 1968 to 1998. TDT maintains this historical information in their Performance History Database. This list appears as in the database with all available information. Some dates do not appear (N/A). The impact of the company on Canadian modern dance is evident after glancing at this impressive roster.

Piece	Choreographer	World Premiere Date
5 Up	Michael Conway	1984-06-07
A Flight of Spiral Stairs	Peter Randazzo	1979-05-19
A Shifting Transparency	Karen duPlessis	1986-04-17
A Simple Melody	Peter Randazzo	1977-10-07
A Thread of Sand	David Earle	1969-12-19
A Walk in Time	Peter Randazzo	1973-10-06
Aftermath	Peter Randazzo	1968-03-18
Against Sleep	Patricia Beatty	1969-02-28
Agitato	Coralee McLaren	1992-03-25
Akhenaten	David Earle	1980-05-15
All Keyed Up	Merle Holloman	1981-03-20
All the Books in Heaven	David Earle	1981-12-19
Amors Gavottes (Original)	Christopher House	1992-10-30
Amors Gavottes	Christopher House	1995-11-07
Ancient Voices of Children	David Earle	1991-04-14
Angelic Visitation #1	David Earle	1968-03-18
Angelic Visitation #2	David Earle	1968-03-18
Animated Shorts	Christopher House	1984-10-16
Antic Eden	Kathryn Brown	1974-03-27
Apollo's Touch	Christopher House	1997-03-11
Arc	Peter Randazzo	1981-11-18
Artemis Madrigals	Christopher House	1988-10-18
Ascension Attended by Lightings	Dennis Highway	1985-05-03
Ashes of Warriors	Sasha Ivanochko	1995-02-01
Atlantis	David Earle	1973-09-25
Attention to Inner Stillness	Phyllis Whyte	1983-04-07
August-Moon	Kathryn Brown	1972-08-09

Piece	Choreographer	World Premiere Date
Aurora	Almond Small	1987-06-25
Autumn Leaves	David Earle	1990-03-06
Babar	Donald Himes	1971-12-27
Back Dance	Danny Grossman	N/A
Balleto al Mio Bel Suon	David Earle	1971-05-10
Banding	Phyllis Whyte	1982-06-01
Barnyard	Christopher House	1993-04-13
Baroque Suite	David Earle	1972-10-03
Baroque Suite (Finale)	David Earle	1973-05-01
Before the Light	Merle Holloman	1984-06-07
Boat, River, Moon	David Earle	1972-10-03
Book of Hours	Christopher House	1995-11-21
Bottari	Christopher House	1997-12-02
Boulevard	Christopher House	1982-06-01
Bugs	David Earle	1974-05-10
Cactus Rosary	Christopher House	1995-03-07
Call Forth the Shades	Finn Martin and Charles Flanders	1980-01-23
Canciones del Alma	Robert Cohan	1979-01-01
Cape Eternity	David Earle	1984-01-01
Capriccio	David Earle	1990-03-06
Caterpillar	Sam Chaiton	1972-08-09
Chant for a Beggar Queen	Ricardo Abreut	1974-03-28
Chiaroscuro	David Earle	1980-09-19
Christmas Concerto	David Earle	1981-12-19
Circles	Luc Tremblay	1985-01-25
Cloud Garden	David Earle	N/A
Colder Ink	Christopher House	1994-04-09
Colouring	Coralee McLaren	1995-02-02
Columbus	Christopher House	1995-03-07
Continuum	Peter Randazzo	1969-12-19
Coronation	Barry Smith	1971-08-01
Couples	Danny Grossman	1976-02-01
Couples Suite	Danny Grossman	1976-01-14
Courances	David Earle	1978-08-15
Court of Miracles	David Earle, Randazzo, House, Anderson, Kudelka	1983-12-15
Courtyard	David Earle	1980-05-07
Craig Dhu	Bill Coleman	1992-11-10
Crosswalk	Laurence Lemieux	1992-03-25
Crystal Palaces	Claudia Moore	1991-03-01
Curious Schools of Theatrical Dancing Pt. 1 (1977)	Danny Grossman	1977-03-02
Dance of the Lepers (Monologue)		1993-11-02

Piece	Choreographer	World Premiere Date
Dark of Moon	Peter Randazzo	1971-05-12
Daybreak	Karen duPlessis	1981-03-26
Debate	Christopher House	1990-03-06
Delicate Pleasures	Christopher House	1994-11-22
Deserteurs	Laurence Lemieux	1993-01-14
Designation Suite:		
Solo	Phyllis Whyte	1982-06-01
Despised	Stephen Beckon	1995-02-01
Deux Epigraphes		
Antiques	David Earle	1975-01-16
Dido and Aeneas	D. Earle,	
	J. Kudelka, C. House,	
	P. Whyte, K. Pearl	1982-07-06
Distant City	Christopher House	1989-09-01
Diversion to		
the Nonexistent		
Enchanted Air		
Gardens	David Rousseve	1985-05-03
Diving for the Moon	David Earle	1992-11-10
Docteurs en		
Vacances	Benoit Lachambre	1984-06-07
Dream in a Dream	Robert Desrosiers	1979-06-29
Dreamsend	David Earle	1990-03-13
Duet	David Hochoy and	
	Dennis Highway	1979-06-20
Duet Untitled	Peter Randazzo	1980-05-14
Eagles Assist		
the Ascension	Dennis Highway	1979-06-20
Early Departures	Christopher House	1992-02-25
Earthbound Angels	Susanna Hood	1995-02-02
Echoes of Honour	Almond Small	1988-04-26
El Amor Brujo	David Earle	1989-07-08
Emerging Ground	Patricia Beatty	1983-09-22
Emotional Geography	David Earle	1985-06-01
Emozioni	David Earle	1980-09-19
En Pantoufles	Karen duPlessis	1987-06-25
Encarnado	Christopher House	1993-07-14
Encounter	Peter Randazzo	1969-05-01
Endless	Rosemary James	1988-04-26
Enter the Dawn	Peter Randazzo	1982-03-23
Evanescence	Miguel Moore	1983-04-07
Exit, Nightfall	David Earle	1981-11-04
Faces	Luc Tremblay	1984-06-07
Faure's Requiem	David Earle	1977-10-21
Field of Dreams	David Earle	1975-02-18
Fifteen (15) Heterosexual		
Duets	James Kudelka	1991-02-22
Figure in the Pit	Peter Randazzo	1973-02-15
Fire in the Eye		
of God	David Earle	1969-02-28
First Music	Patricia Beatty	1969-05-01

Piece	Choreographer	World Premiere Date
Independence Day	Bill Coleman	1998-03-11
Isis and Nefertari	Claudia Moore	1979-06-22
Island	Christopher House	1989-03-28
It's Magic When You're in Love	Sam Chaiton	1972-08-08
Jour de nuit	Luc Tremblay	1982-06-01
Journee à la Plage	Bill Coleman	1992-03-25
Journey	David Earle	1981-12-19
L'Appartement	Janet Aronoff	1985-05-03
L'Assassin Menace	Peter Randazzo	1975-01-10
L'Aureole Bleue	David Pressault	1992-03-25
L'Histoire du Soldat	Martin Brenzell	1971-02-01
L'Hiver Dernier	Laurence Lemieux	1997-03-11
L'Hotel Splendide	David Earle	1975-01-16
La Bilancia	David Earle	1980-09-19
La Bilancia (original)	Graham Jackson, Jeannie Teillet, Grace Miyagawa	1980-01-24
Lady Fox	Barry Smith	1971-08-01
Lament	David Earle	N/A
Landscape with Figures	Christopher House	1983-11-10
Las Primas	Ricardo Abreut	1980-01-23
Leaving You My Hand Me Downs	Michael Sean Marye	1988-04-26
Logond	David Earle	1971-05-12
Les Orphelins	Claudia Moore	1980-01-23
Les Seins de Pierre	Pascal Desrosiers	1993-01-14
Lessons in Another Language	Patricia Beatty	1980-05-07
Let the Spirit Move Yah	Almond Small	1987-06-25
Los Sencillos	Patricia Beatty	1972-10-12
Lover and Lesser Man	David Wood	1974-03-27
Lovers	David Earle	1969-02-28
Lyrical Solo	David Earle	1972-03-20
Maelstrom	David Earle	1996-05-08
Mahalia	Wendy Chiles	1979-06-20
Mandala	Patricia Beatty	1992-02-25
Maneuvers	Karen duPlessis	1984-06-07
Mantis	Christopher House	1979-06-20
Mas'hara	Patricia Beatty	1981-09-11
Medley	Suzette Sherman	1981-03-20
Midnight Faune	Barry Smith	1974-03-27
Mind Running Upon	Colleen May	1972-08-08
Mirrors	David Earle	1968-12-02
Moments Like This	Rosemary James	1992-03-25
Momentum	Patricia Beatty	1967-12-01
Moon	Nancy Ferguson	1979-06-20
Moonchase	David Earle	1981-03-26

Piece	Choreographer	World Premiere Date
Moving to Drumming	Peter Randazzo	1980-05-07
Mythic Journey	Peter Randazzo	1974-05-10
Mythos	David Earle	1977-12-14
Namaskar	Chandralekha	1997-12-08
National Spirit	Danny Grossman	1976-01-14
Nighthawks	Peter Randazzo	1976-04-27
Nimrod	Donald Himes	1975-07-09
Nocturnal Visions	Naoko Murakoshi	N/A
Noli Me Tangere	Christopher House	1991-06-05
Nothing for Something	Nancy Ferguson	1978-09-19
O Saisons. O Chateaux	Clover Roope	1969-02-16
Oasis	Jane Stephen	1974-03-28
Octet	Peter Randazzo	1981-05-16
Ode	Kale Alton	1993-01-14
Office Suite	Charles Flanders	1980-01-24
Om Los Te Laat	Rosemary James	1993-01-14
Ome	David Pressault	1993-01-14
Openings and Inventions	David Earle	1990-06-10
Operetta	David Earle	1970-05-09
Opus #4	David Hochoy	1979-06-20
Or Liquide	Benoit Lachambre and the dancers	1987-06-25
Ormai	David Earle	1982-03-07
Orphic Construction	Christopher House	1981-03-26
Outside in Time	Peter Randazzo	1990-03-06
Over the Rainbow	Jeannie Teillet	1979-06-20
Palace of Pleasure	David Earle	1988-04-05
Paladin Vespers	Christopher House	1997-03-11
Parade	David Earle	1974-11-14
Passage from Memory	Merle Holloman	1985-12-13
Patient Cherubs	Michael Trent	1993-01-14
Pendently	Karen duPlessis	1980-01-24
Père à Louer	Pascal Desrosiers	1995-02-02
Phrases from Orpheus		1971-06-11
Pie Jesu		1970-12-15
Pierce	Peter Chin	1997-03-11
Pingo Slink	Christopher House	1996-02-28
Pocamania	Kathryn Brown	1972-08-08
Portrait	David Earle	1970-10-14
Postscript	Susan Macpherson	1971-10-15
Preambule	Laurence Lemieux	1987-06-25
Precipice	Susanna Hood	1993-01-14
Primordial	Grant Strate	1968-11-01
Private Dancer	Learie McNicolls	1986-04-17
Prospect Park	Peter Randazzo	1971-05-14

Piece	Choreographer	World Premiere Date
Quartet.	David Earle	1976-04-09
Queen Bee	Odette Oliver	1974-03-28
Quodlibet.	Christopher House and David Earle	1990-03-06
Radical Light	Patricia Beatty.	1986-07-01
Raptures and Ravings	Patricia Beatty.	1983-09-22
Raven	David Earle	N/A
Ray Charles Suite	David Earle	1973-03-01
Re'em	Karen duPlessis	1979-06-22
Realm	David Earle	1983-03-24
Recital	Peter Randazzo	1977-03-04
Rejoice in the Lamb.	David Earle and Nancy Ferguson	1979-03-30
Resolve.	Merle Holloman	1983-04-07
Rewind.	Peter Randazzo	1985-02-09
Rhapsody in the Late Afternoon	Patricia Beatty.	1971-05-14
Rite for Future Time.	Patricia Beatty.	1983-02-23
Romance	David Earle	1990-03-06
Ruby	David Earle	1973-03-01
Sacra Conversazione	David Earle	1984-07-01
Sacred Garden	David Earle	1986-02-01
Sang.	David Earle, Sean Marye and the Company.	1996-12-10
Scherzo.	Christopher House.	1989-10-07
Schola Cantorum	Christopher House.	1981-03-08
Schubert Dances.	Christopher House.	1985-09-26
Seastill	Patricia Beatty.	1979-04-25
Secrets That Belong to the Night.	Michael Conway	1983-04-07
Shadow of our Former Selves.	Anna Blewchamp (Peter Randazzo)	1981-05-12
Shibboleth	Graham McKelvie.	1992-03-25
Sisu	Michael Trent	1995-02-01
Skyling.	Patricia Beatty.	1980-07-26
Snakes and Ladders (A Study)	Learie McNicolls	1985-05-03
Soli Representativa	Michael Trent.	1992-03-25
Solo and Trio for Two	Clover Roope	1969-02-16
Solo Beyond the Breathing Place.	Christopher Bannerman.	1978-09-19
Song	Billyann Balay.	1981-03-26
Songs from the Newfoundland Outports.	Donald Himes	1971-05-10
Spatstil	Peggy Baker	1992-09-26
Spirits of Sadness Depart.	Phyllis Whyte	1981-12-19

Piece	Choreographer	World Premiere Date
Sports et Divertissements	Christopher House	1981-03-08
Starscape	Peter Randazzo	1971-05-13
Stolen Thunder	Nancy Ferguson	1980-01-24
Study for a Song in the Distance	Patricia Beatty	1969-12-18
Suite Hope	Jeannie Teillet	1979-05-01
Suite Saturday Night	Suzette Sherman	1980-01-24
Summer Evening	Peter Randazzo	1992-11-10
Sunrise	David Earle	1987-01-01
Sunwapta	Keith Urban	1971-05-14
Sweet and Low Down	David Earle	1979-09-01
Table Dances	Andrew Giday	1995-02-01
Tango	Kate Alton	1995-02-01
Tango, So!	Peter Randazzo	1982-03-25
Tex Made	Wendy Chiles	1979-06-22
The Amber Garden	Peter Randazzo	1972-03-20
The Chair Pieces V Enders	Murray Darroch	1981-03-08
The Clay Forest	David Earle	1992-08-01
The Court of Lions	Christopher House	1990-03-13
The Dream	Karen duPlessis	1988-04-26
The Excitable Gift	Christopher House	1982-05-04
The Lacemakers	Barry Smith	1972-03-21
The Last Act	Peter Randazzo	1972-10-12
The Last Dance	Peter Randazzo	1981-11-18
The Letter	Peter Randazzo	1974-10-30
The Light Brigade	Peter Randazzo	1979-04-25
The Nutcrackershitsuite Part 1	Ron Ladd	1987-06-25
The Opening	Patricia Beatty	1969-02-28
The Painter's Dream	David Earle	1993-12-10
The Recitation	David Earle	1968-03-18
The Reprieve	Patricia Beatty	1975-05-23
The Silent Feast	David Earle	1971-10-19
The Survival Suite	Learie McNicolls	1987-06-25
The Third Awakening	Barry Smith	1973-05-19
The Visit	Merle Holloman	1985-05-03
The Wedding Duet	David Earle	1979-01-01
The Windows	Christopher House	1988-12-01
Think of One	Learie McNicolls	1987-06-25
Three Sided Room	Peter Randazzo	1972-10-06
Three Songs	Michael Kraus	1986-04-17
Threshold	Patricia Beatty	1991-04-16
Thunder Contained	Susanna Hood	1992-03-25
Tidings	Almond Small	1988-04-26
Tompkin Square	Mitch Kirsch	1979-06-22
Torn Picture	Michael Conway	1982-06-01
Toss Quintet	Christopher House	1980-05-07

Piece	Choreographer	World Premiere Date
Trapezoid.	Peter Randazzo	1968-12-02
Triad	Donald Himes	1972-08-09
Triumph of Love	David Earle	1988-11-08
Two Renaissance Songs.	Christopher House and David Earle	1990-04-21
Two Women	Susan Macpherson.	1980-01-24
Unblinking	Phyllis Whyte	1982-06-01
Unruffled Lake.	Graham McKelvie	1993-01-14
Untitled (Coleman).	Bill Coleman	1993-01-14
Untitled (Flanders).	Charles Flanders	1979-06-22
Untitled	Susan Macpherson.	1975-07-09
Untitled (May)	Colleen May	1971-12-01
Untitled Dance	Keith Urban	1970-02-22
Untitled Monument.	David Earle	1992-02-25
Untitled Quartet.	Christopher House.	1984-05-03
Untitled Solo	Peter Randazzo	1970-10-22
Valse à Deux Temps.	Laurence Lemieux.	1988-04-26
Vestige	Marie Josee Chartier.	1998-03-11
Vignette	David Earle	1975-01-16
Villagerie	Luc Tremblay	1983-04-07
Visible Distance: A Bach Suite	David Earle	1992-07-03
Visions for a Theatre of the Mind	Peter Randazzo	1971-09-01
Vivaldi	Peter Randazzo	1988-04-06
Voyage for Four Male Dancers	Peter Randazzo	1970-05-26
Waiting.	Kathryn Brown.	1976-07-24
Waltz Suite	David Earle	1975-01-16
Wasichu.	Kathy Wildberger	1971-05-01
What You See is What You Get.	Elaine Bowman	1974-03-28
What's Your Name?	Sylvie Bouchard	1988-04-26
WILLAWARNOCK SSONSINGS.	Ron Ladd	1988-04-26
Words and Movements for individuals	Benoît Lachambre.	1985-05-03
Work in Progress	Coralee McLaren	1993-01-14
Wretched Ha! Ha!	Odette Oliver	1974-03-27
Yesterday	David Earle	1973-03-01
You, Yoo and Me.	Monica Burr	1987-06-25
Zefiro Torna	Christopher House.	1990-03-29

Notes

Chapter One
Trish Beatty

p. 1   ... If we can't do what we want with passion....
Herbert Whittaker, "Boom Time For Modern Dancers," *The Globe and Mail*, 10 May 1969, p. 24.

p. 1   ... It is a way of communicating that gives dignity....
Peggy Baker, 1998.

p. 2   ... must own a bowling alley....
Peter Randazzo, 1992.

p. 2   ... purple tights and a purple leotard....
David Earle, 1992.

p. 2   ... Every modern dancer knew each other in the city....
Sandy Naiman, "Still Some Dance In Me," *The Toronto Sun*, 19 September 1983, p. 37.

Lilian Jarvis had been dancing with the National Ballet but wanted more from dance. She received one of the first Canada Council grants to study modern at the Martha Graham School of Contemporary Dance....

p. 3   I was born to save my mother's life....
Trish Beatty, 1998.

p. 3   ... I felt more than this 'good little girl'...
Trish Beatty, 1998.

Gladys Forrester was a Toronto dancer and ballet teacher of the Royal Academy of Dancing method. Many Canadian dancers were trained by her. She was recipient of Dance Ontario Award in 1995, and the Royal Academy of Dancing President's Award in London England in January 1998. She died suddenly in March 1998, two weeks after Nadine Saxton spoke with her.

p. 4   ... a lovely mover, she had great expression....
Conversation with Gladys Forrester, 1998.

p. 4   ... I knew I didn't belong in classical dance....
Trish Beatty, 1998.

Bennington College had begun as a progressive liberal arts college for undergraduate women in 1932. It was, as Beatty stated, "a creative experiment in education." Martha Hill, a former member of Martha Graham's early "Group," was instrumental in the establishment of the Bennington School of the Dance in 1934. The school became famous for its intensive summer training courses that brought modern greats Martha Graham, Doris Humphrey, Charles Weidman, and Hanya Holm to the campus, each to teach a session, as well as create new works on the students. In addition to technique, the school offered courses in dance composition, stage design, music, and dance criticism. Many

Bennington teachers and students went on to head dance departments and form companies for experimental work all over the United States and throughout the world. [Agnes De Mille, *Martha: The Life and Works of Martha Graham* (New York: Random House, 1991), 203–206.]

p. 4　　...My teachers put me through a tough verbal examination....
　　　　Patricia Beatty, *Form Without Formula*, Toronto: Press of Terpsichore Ltd., 1989, p. 56.

Pearl Lang joined Martha Graham's company in 1941 and remained there until 1952 when she formed her own company. When Graham relinquished some of her roles, they went to Lang. Lang is "generally considered one of the leading modern dancers and is acclaimed everywhere for her beauty and the mastery of her dancing." De Mille, 1991: 461. According to Beatty, in the sixties, dance auditions were only for Broadway: by taking classes and being seen, young modern dancers were asked to work with established choreographers. It was this process that led to Beatty's association with Lang.

p. 5　　... She used her torso in a way that I believe....
　　　　Trish Beatty, 1998.

p. 5　　... I was unorthodox when it came to teaching children....
　　　　Trish Beatty 1998.

p. 5　　... You were a war veteran....
　　　　Trish Beatty, 1992, 1998.

p. 6　　... I have found a place for you to teach....
　　　　Trish Beatty, 1992.

p. 6　　... artists need enough money....
　　　　Trish Beatty, 1998.

p. 7　　... Can you imagine? Glass changing rooms!...
　　　　Trish Beatty, 1992.

p. 7　　... My family were a little awkward about me....
　　　　Trish Beatty, 1998.

p. 9　　... Modern dance repertory company... The first performance work for the company was a television series for the Anglican Church ...
　　　　Personal letter to Jillian Officer

As her reputation grew, Beatty was invited across Canada to teach movement courses in such places as Drumheller and Edmonton, Alberta, Northern Ontario, and Halifax.

Most of the dancers in the company were still training, and Torontonians had little exposure to dance types other than ballet. For these reasons the opportunities to perform were limited.

p. 9　　... I was making all the decisions... when the curtain rose....
　　　　Trish Beatty, 1998.

David Earle

As soon as Hitler invaded Poland in September 1939, France and England declared war on Germany. The "phoney war" in England refers to the period of time from September 1939 to May 1940 when no British were actively fighting. After Germany invaded Holland, Belgium, and France, Prime Minister Chamberlain stepped down and Churchill took over in time to engage Hitler at Dunkirk.

p. 10　　... I attempted to be a peace maker....
　　　　"Reshaping A Vision," *Vandance International*, Fall 1992: 10–13.

p. 11   ... pseudo-gothic United Church... I think it is the stone, the glass, the music, the poetry, ...
David Earle, 1998.

p. 12   ... Everything that is good in me....
David Earle, 1998.

Helen and Fanny Birdsall... Dance Collection Danse

p. 12   ... My first ballets were button ballets....
David Earle, 1998.

Toronto Children's Players information from conversations with former members of the Toronto Children's Players, Martin and Judy Hunter, Summer 1998

p. 13   ... We were in terror of her....
David Earle, 1998.

p. 13   ... Make-up was a great inspiration... imagine four times a year... I found tremendous Eros....
David Earle, 1998.

p. 14   ... Image addict....
David Earle, 1998.

p. 14   ... I was a special student...
David Earle, 1992.

p. 14   ... music, unbelievably refreshing....
David Earle, 1992.

Dalcroze Eurythmics is a system for learning musical rhythms through movement.
"turns around the back" — a Graham technique exercise sitting upright on the floor, the sit bones remain connected to the floor as one turns or spirals as far as possible to the right or left arm movements are involved.

p. 15   ... of course we cannot teach you to dance ....
David Earle, 1998.

Danny Grossman danced for ten years with the Paul Taylor dance company before emigrating to Canada. He later danced with the Toronto Dance Theatre before forming his own company in 1978.
    Jamie Cunningham remained in New York and founded his own company, ACME Dance Theatre.

p. 16   ... that's how we met....
David Earle, 1998.

p. 16   ... I went to lawyers....
David Earle, 1992.

p. 16   ... Christ the King Cathedral... Living conditions....
David Earle, 1998.

Peter Randazzo

p. 17   ... Totally insecure... where it becomes very tribal....
Peter Randazzo, 1992.

p. 18   ... He could do all this amazing stuff.... I would literally tear my body apart... I wasn't particularly interested in doing [Graham's] work....
Peter Randazzo, 1992.

p. 18   ... every time I opened my mouth... Graham's greatest gift was to show you "you".
Peter Randazzo, 1992.

Martha Graham created parts for Randazzo in: *Secular Games, Legend of Judith, Circe, The Witch of Endor, Part Real Part Dream, Dancing Ground, The Plain of Prayer, The Lady of the House of Sleep, Cortege of Eagles.* Other works Randazzo danced in: *Diversion of Angels, Alcestra, Clytemnestra, Phaedra.* Randazzo's other dance training includes ballet with Antony Tudor, Robert Joffrey, Leon Danielian, and Madame Swoboda.

p. 19   ... My rent was $71 a month....
Peter Randazzo, 1992.

p. 20   ... The reason we didn't get along....
Peter Randazzo, 1992.

p. 20   ... We had a Clytemnestra rehearsal....
Peter Randazzo, 1992.

p. 22   ... Well, you certainly are the dancer....
Donald Himes, 1998.

p. 22   ... like I belong here....
Peter Randazzo, 1998.

p. 22   ... Let's start a dance company....
Peter Randazzo, 1992.

Chapter Two

The Formation of Toronto Dance Theatre
Beatty was 32, Earle was 29, and Randazzo was 26 at the time of the formation.

p. 23   ... I was teaching so much and I was fund-raising....
Trish Beatty, 1998.

p. 24   ... gracious to accept....
David Earle, 1992.

p. 24   ... Kenny Pearl was my only regular student.
David Earle, 1992, 1998.

p. 25   ... They called me and said would I like to come back ... they were exciting times.
Susan Macpherson, 1992.

In December 1968 the three Mondays were, 2, 9, 16. Dancers were, Peter, Trish, David, Kevin McGarrigle, Donald Himes, Barry (now Artis) Smith, Merle (now Germaine) Salsberg, Amelia Itcush, and Susan Macpherson. Keith Urban, Kathy Wildberger, Norrey Drummond were soon to join the company. Donald Himes would continue to guest with the company, but Kevin McGarrigle left after the first season.

Making It All a Bit More "Legitimate"
Blue laws refer laws governing social activities such as Sunday shopping and the hours for the consumption of alcohol.

p. 25   ... very cute....
Peter Randazzo, 1998.

p. 26   ... It was a beautiful time....
Peggy Baker, 1998.

p. 26   ... foundation of the organization....
Trish Beatty, 1992.

p. 26   ... they made us feel that the community had an appetite for us....
David Earle, 1992.

p. 26   ... I think we wanted to produce a company that would...
David Earle, 1992.

p. 27   ... I'm not interested in something new....
David Earle, 1998.

p. 27   ... What has brought the Toronto Dance Theatre to such notice... We all differ in choreography....
Herbert Whittaker, "Boom Time For Modern Dancers," *The Globe and Mail* 10 May 1969, p. 24.

p. 28   ... *Lovers...* is more complex....
Ralph Hicklin, "A Lightning Tour De Force By Toronto Dance Theatre," *Toronto Telegram*, 2 May 1969, p. 72.

p. 28   ... eloquent simplicity
Nathan Cohen, "Our Dance Theatre the Most Stunning In the Country," *Toronto Daily Star*, 27 May 1970, p. 36.

p. 28   ... pure sustained movement without a thought of any emotion behind it....
Lawrence O'Toole, "New Choreography Allows TDT Breathing Space," *The Globe and Mail*, 6 December 1976, p. 16.

p. 29   . Miss Beatty [has] established a new stature for herself....
Hicklin, 1969.

p. 29   ... Because all three choreographers were so different...,
Paula Citron, "Talking With Susan Macpherson," *Dance in Canada*, Summer 1986, p. 23.

Inky Fingers

p. 30   ... The company really runs on a democratic ethic....
Barbara Gail Rowes, "Toronto Dance Theatre," *Dance Magazine*, April 1971: 70–72.

p. 31   ... Like a little hippy tribe....
Peggy Baker, 1998.

p. 31   ... We were very "in" with the hippies we knew... It was a smash....
Trish Beatty, 1998.

Trish's marriage lasted six years.

p. 31   ... Peter is very good with facts and figures....
David Earle, 1992.

p. 31   ... I taught classes, made costumes, rehearsed....
Paula Citron, "Talking With Susan Macpherson," *Dance in Canada*, Summer 1986: 22.

p. 31   ... We couldn't have started if we hadn't personally known....
Herbert Whittaker, "Boom Time For Modern Dancers," *The Globe and Mail*, 10 May 1969, p. 24.

p. 31   ... We always had ink on our hands....
David Earle, 1992.

p. 32   ... Father supported Toronto Dance Theatre...
Clifford Beatty, 1992.

p. 32   ... I realized it was a full-time job....
Trish Beatty, 1992.

p. 32   ... did everything but make laundry and make costumes....
James Plaxton, 1992.

James Plaxton's background did not include administration. He had apprenticed with an architectural firm in Winnipeg before moving to Toronto in 1965, where he worked as a freelance design artist. Plaxton was interested in film and by 1968 was working at Cinecity, a film and theatre establishment at the corner of Yonge and Charles Street. One of the ushers at the theatre was Amelia Itcush, a dancer with the Toronto Dance Theatre. Itcush suggested he design a set for one of the directors of the company and introduced him to Peter Randazzo. Plaxton designed and built the set for *Encounter* which was performed in May 1969 at the MacMillan Theatre during the company's first season. [James Plaxton, 1992.]

The university circuit included: The University of Toronto, York University, McMaster University, Brock University, University of Guelph, University of Waterloo, University of Western Ontario.

"Our Guy" in Charge

p. 33   ... Everyone had lots of ballet but if you had a scholarship at
TDT.... If you were a serious student....
Peggy Baker, 1998.

p. 33   ... Freedom Hall....
Trish Beatty, 1998.

p. 34   ... I didn't know much about dance....
Ron Snippe, 1998.

Ron Snippe joined TDT as lighting designer in 1973. He has filled many other roles over the years with the company such as technical director, stage manager, and company manager. At the time of writing, he remains with TDT.

"The Place" to Be
The Place Theatre is the home of the London Contemporary Dance Theatre.

p. 35   ... Peter Randazzo, the most Grahamized....
Craig Dodd, "Toronto Dance Theatre," *The Dancing Times*,
Spring 1972: 417.

Company dancers at The Place were: Peter Trish David, Susan Macpherson, Barry (Artis) Smith, Amelia Itcush, Merle (Germaine) Salsberg, Kathy Wildberger, Helen Jones, Norrey Drummond, David Wood, Donald Himes.

Fame without Fortune
Graham Jackson is a writer who has been associated with Toronto Dance Theatre almost since its inception. He worked as a librarian around the corner from their first studio on Cumberland Street. Particularly in the 1970s, Jackson reviewed and wrote about the company for *Dance in Canada* and newspapers. He has collaborated with David Earle and remained a long time objective supporter of the company. He now practices as a Jungian psychoanalyst.

p. 36   ... People were crazy about this company....
Peggy Baker, 1998.

p. 37   ... She wore Birkenstocks....
Peggy Baker, 1998.

p. 37   ... He was like walking electricity....
Peggy Baker, 1998.

p. 38   ... They would never listen to each other....
Donald Himes, 1998.

Toronto Workshop Productions was a small theatre, located at Yonge and Alexander Streets. Today the venue houses Buddies in Bad Times, run by Skye Gilbert.

p. 38   ... People were crazed when they got there....
Peggy Baker, 1998.

New Dances and Nudity

p. 39   ... A dancer inside a cloth tube...
cited in Jillian Officer, "Works which appear in the repertoire of Toronto Dance Theatre," unpublished 1980, TDT Archives.

p. 39   One of the security staff....
David Earle, Peter Randazzo, 1998

p. 40   ... with the inevitability of fashion, nudity hit the....
Herbert Whittaker cited in Officer, 1980.

p. 40   ... Some pretty groovy hips....
Barbara Gail Rowes, "Troupe Stresses Sense Of Spoof," *The Globe and Mail* 8 January 1971, p. 12.

p. 41   ... And what a chorus....
William Littler, *The Toronto Star*, 20 May 1971, cited in Officer, 1980.

p. 41   ... is a lyric fantasy with an element of surrealism....
William Littler, *The Toronto Star* 14 October 1971, cited in Officer, 1980.

p. 42   ... has all the hallmarks of a classic creation....
John Fraser, *The Globe and Mail,* cited in Officer, 1980.

p. 43   ... Divine... the relations that were going on in the company....
Trish Beatty, 1998.

p. 43   ... A comical look at the erotic fantasies which occupy...
cited in Officer, 1980.

Gloom and Doom and Taking a Bow

p. 43   ... Must everything be serious....
Ralph Hicklin, "A Lightning Tour De Force By Toronto Dance Theatre," *Toronto Telegram*, 2 May 1969, p. 72.

p. 43   ... It is obvious....
Barbara Gail Rowes, "Dance Steps Backward to Find New Inspiration in Its Origins," *The Globe and Mail*, 29 March 1971, p. 13.

p. 43   ... shadow of Graham's approaches....
Selma Landen Odom, "New Homes for Dance in Toronto," *Performing Arts in Canada*, Summer 1973: 41–42.

p. 44   ... There was a huge initial response....
David Earle, 1992.

p. 44   ... going out of their minds....
Peggy Baker, 1998.

p. 45 ...We have to honour that....
Trish Beatty, 1998.

p. 45 ... tired of sacred, classical, religious experiences....
James Plaxton, 1992.

Babar

p. 46 ... at one time when the name Toronto Dance Theatre....
Donald Himes, 1998.

p. 46 ... When I was in the professional programme ...
written for this book by Susan Cash, 1998.

Reality Strikes Again

p. 47 ... The company's biggest problem....
John Fraser, "Financial Troubles for Dance Theatre," *The Globe and Mail*, 21 October 1972, p. 26.

By April 1973, the staff consisted of an administrator, musical director, resident composer, production/publicity manager, technical director, technical assistant, wardrobe supervisor, two resident musicians and a school coordinator. Dancers in the company were Peter, Trish, David, Susan Macpherson, Barry (Artis) Smith, Merle (Germaine) Salsberg, Helen Jones, David Wood, Kathryn Brown, John Preston, Norrey Drummond, guest artist Danny Grossman, and apprentices, Peggy Baker, Patricia Miner, Sara Pettitt, Jane Foster.

Chapter Three

p. 49 ... When do you ever feel secure....
Stephen Godfrey, "Following the Steps of TDT," *The Globe and Mail*, 14 August 1978, p. 11.

p. 50 ... sort of post-ballet moment....
Jennifer Fisher, "From Post-Ballet to Post-Modern: Revisiting the Debut Concert of Toronto's Fifteen Dance Collective, June 13, 1972," *Canadian Dance Studies I 1994*, edited by Selma Odom and Mary Jane Warner, Graduate Programme in Dance, York University, p. 169.

The Managing Director

p. 51 ... I took a hard look at where the funding was coming from....
Roger Jones, 1992.

p. 52 ... After he arrived....
David Earle, 1992.

The School

p. 53 ... People would take class without paying....
Graham Jackson, "Graham Training Settles In Canada," *Dance in Canada* Summer 1977: 21–24.

Professionalism and (Sniff) "Amateurs"

p. 53 ... there was a lot of other things percolating....
Peggy Baker, 1998.

p. 54 ... We had tremendous battles about the Graham technique....
Donald Himes, 1998.

p. 54 ... those were down years for TDT....
Peggy Baker, 1998.

Grant Auditions

p. 54   ... How would they know how to evaluate....
Trish Beatty, 1998.

p. 55   ... It's a good thing he did because I got the grant.... TDT was
the only modern dance....
Peggy Baker, 1998.

p. 55   ... More disheartening is the betrayal....
Graham Jackson, "Martha's Web: Ten Years with Toronto
Dance Theatre," *Dance in Canada*, Winter 1978–79: 3–8.

Lightning Does Not Strike Twice: The Second International Tour

p. 56   ... The dancers were not used to a raked stage....
Roger Jones, 1992.

p. 56   ... Critics Pan Toronto Dance Theatre....
James Anderson, "Critics Pan Toronto," *The Globe and Mail*,
27 June 1974, p. 14.

p. 56   ... We were horrified....
David Earle, 1992.

p. 57   ... violent and public curses....
John Fraser, "The Summer of 1974: Memories (mostly bad) for
Toronto Dance Theatre," *The Globe and Mail*, 10 August 1974.

Company members for this tour were: Peter, David, Susan Macpherson, Barry (Artis) Smith, Merle (Germaine) Salsberg, Helen Jones, Norrey Drummond, David Wood, Kathryn Brown, Danny Grossman, John Peston, Ricardo Abreut, musician, apprentices, Peggy Baker, Sara Pettitt, Pat Miner, Cornelius Fisher-Credo.

Suiting Up

p. 57   ... He said, 'I want to see someone in a suit....'
David Earle, 1992.

Touring is a paradox that most dance companies face. In 1973, McKinsey and Co. state in *Directions for the Dance* that touring is "essential for increasing the audience base, expanding revenues and for lengthening the season." The paradox is that the high cost of touring greatly outweighs the gains. [McKinsey and Co. *Directions for the Dance in Canada* Ottawa; Canada Council, 1973: 2–5.]

The company made the following tours. 1974–75 failed European tour, Eastern Canada, Western Canada; in 1976 Montreal Olympic Games, Toronto Dance Festival; 1977, Eastern Canada.

Creating the Work: Two

p. 58   ... has always seemed especially sensitive to....
Graham Jackson. "Martha's Web: Ten Years with Toronto
Dance Theatre." *Dance in Canada* Winter 1978–79: 3–8.

p. 59   ... I don't think I ever missed a rehearsal....
Karen duPlessis, 1998.

p. 59   ... Randazzo does not push any solutions....
John Fraser, *The Globe and Mail*, cited from Officer, Jillian
"Works which appear in the Repertoire of Toronto Dance Thea-
tre," unpublished 1980, TDT Archives.

p. 59   ... takes swipes at high fashion....
Graham Jackson, "Martha's Web...," *Dance in Canada*, Winter
1978–79: 3–8.

p. 59   ... *Bugs*, a work in four parts....
         cited in Jillian Officer, "Works which appear in the Repertoire
         of Toronto Dance Theatre," unpublished 1980, TDT Archives.

p. 60   ... Phaedra's crime is her choice of lovers....
         David Earle, Programme notes, TDT Archives, 1979.

p. 60   ... David is a nineteenth century soul....
         Trish Beatty, 1998.

Danny

p. 61   ... although the association has been a mutually satisfying
         one....
         Graham Jackson, "Martha's Web: Ten Years With Toronto
         Dance Theatre," *Dance in Canada*, Winter 1978–79: 3–8.

The Times They Are a 'Changin'

Lindsay Kemp was a performance artist based in England who had
great success when he brought his company to Toronto Workshop Productions theatre in 1970s.

p. 63   ... Community was integral....
         Suzette Sherman, 1998.

p. 64   ... A kind of happy but efficient anarchy exists....
         Michael Crabb, "Dance Theatre Does What It Believes in," *The
         Toronto Star*, 15 May 1976, p. D9.

The Toronto Dance Festival of 1976
and the Good Times

The "Silver Seven" refers to the companies that were receiving substan-
tial funding from the Canada Council; Les Grands Ballets Canadiens,
The National Ballet of Canada, the National Ballet School, Toronto
Dance Theatre, The Royal Winnipeg Ballet, Winnipeg Contemporary
Dancers, Anna Wyman Dance Theatre.

Despite the "down times," in 1973 the company received $70,250 in
grants. In 1974, the grants more than doubled to $191,100. By 1976,
this figure had risen to total $329,410.

Toronto Dance Theatre received $70,000 from the Canada Council
in 1975 and $100,000 in 1976.

1976 Company dancers were Peter, Trish, David, guests, Danny
Grossman, Kathryn Brown, Susan Macpherson, Sara Pettitt, Jean-Louis
Morin, Nancy Ferguson, Dennis Highway, Chuck Flanders, Dindi Lidge,
Claudia Moore, Jan Messer, Dale Woodland, Judy Hendin, Eric Bobrow,
Greg Parks.

"... Authority Patterns Are
Like Child-Parent Roles"

p. 65   ... authority patterns are like child-parent roles....
         Stephen Godfrey, "Following TDT's Steps," *The Globe and
         Mail*, 14 August 1978, p. 11.

p. 66   ... I think partly what happened there....
         Peggy Baker, 1998.

"... and Not Interfere Artistically"

p. 66   ... meddle in artistic decisions.... "We had tremendous rows
         over things publicity said...."
         Roger Jones, 1992.

The Tenth Anniversary

p. 69   ... the consciousness of not sticking to one style.... I look at some of my earlier choreography....
Stephen Godfrey, "Following TDT's Steps," *The Globe and Mail*, 14 August 1978, p. 11.

p. 70   ... I felt I was able to give Peter and David strength....
Trish Beatty, 1998.

p. 70   ... I feel we've been barely begun....
Stephen Godfrey, 1978.

Company dancers for the anniversary were: Peter Sparling (guesting from the Martha Graham Dance Company who later did not go on tour with TDT), Peter, David, Susan Macpherson, Claudia Moore, Nancy Ferguson, Wendy Chiles, Dennis Highway (left after this season to work with Clive Thompson who had guested in April) Charles Flanders, Keith Urban, David Wood, Suzette Sherman, Sherry Lanier, Karen duPlessis, Jeannie Teillet, Grace Miyagawa, Mitchell Kirsch, Christopher House.

Chapter Four

p. 73   ... They left for the same reasons I left Pearl Lang's company....
Stephen Godfrey, "Dance Theatre Alive and Kicking in Cabbagetown," *The Globe and Mail*, 7 October 1980, p. F7.

Keeping Three Balls in the Air

p. 74   ... they [the founders] knew they had someone really good,...
Peggy Baker, 1998.

Roger Jones was in charge of the renovations. "When he built the building, he didn't build any place for Peter, Trish, and me. He had two corner offices, one for his secretary and one for himself. He had the tower to relax in, as a retreat with bookshelves and carpet ... so when we came here we said "Well Roger, where are we supposed to go?" ... He said, "Where would you like to be?" We said, "Well, what's left?" So we said we'd take the tower because we needed somewhere to retreat. [David Earle, 1992.]

p. 74   ... along for the ride....
Clifford Beatty, 1992.

p. 74   ... we'd done the whole thing....
Roger Jones, 1992.

The membership of this board retained many of the people from the advisory board. in 1979, the board consisted of Clifford Beatty, Douglas Earle, the founders, Roger Jones, Harry Malcolmson, senior partner with the law firm of Rosenfeld Malcolmson, and Beth Jones. By 1980, the board had recruited David Atkins, senior partner of Coopers & Lybrand, David Andrus, president of Dominion Securities Investment Advisory Services, Christine Forsythe, corporate affairs officer of Sun Life Assurance, and composer Ann Southam. When the school and the company split, Beth Robinson left the company board to become the president of the board for the School of Toronto Dance Theatre.

    Clifford Beatty, President of the Board, explains he "was along for the ride" and the board did not see or approve budgets until after Roger left.

Creating the Work: Three

p. 75   ... *Seastill* was the first piece I did after two years of not dancing....
Trish Beatty, cited in Jillian Officer, "Works which appear in the Repertoire of Toronto Dance Theatre," unpublished 1980, TDT Archives.

p. 75   ... Trish is unlike anybody else....
Karen duPlessis, 1998.

p. 75   ... a mellifluous soporific....
Stephen Godfrey, *The Globe and Mail*, cited in Officer, 1980.

p. 75   ... The first time we did *Lessons*....
cited in Officer, 1980.

p. 76   ... A delicious and ambivalent work....
William Littler, *The Toronto Star*, cited in Officer, 1980.

p. 77   ... A work of filigree detail so openly and eloquently wrought....
Alina Gildiner, "Earle Feature Covers Wide Range," *The Globe and Mail*, 17 February 1983, p. 24.

p. 77   ... a different Randazzo who peddled pain and exposure....
William Littler, *The Toronto Star*, cited in Officer, 1980.

p. 77   ... I still have a jar of pennies at home....
David Earle, 1998.

p. 78   ... represented newer dancers....
Denis Joffre, 1998.

Un Certaine Âge

Title for section taken from Stephen Godfrey, "TDT Seeks Fairy Godmother To Solve Its Mid-Life Crisis," *The Globe and Mail*, 3 May 1980, p. E7.

    GAMI's use of the term "post-modern" is historical, and refers to the fact that TDT was considered "traditional" modern dance for some presenters.

p. 79   ... It is apparent from the point of view of your artistic directors....
letter from Peter Sever, president of GAMI, to Roger Jones, 20 May 1981, TDT Archives.

p. 80   ... The theatre has experienced significant losses...
audited financial statement 1981, TDT Archives.

The "Disaster Specialist"

At the time of his appointment to Toronto Dance Theatre, Ed had worked as an executive assistant to the director of marketing for CBC Radio and Television, and vice-president and general manager of Haber Artists. He also had worked as grant coordinator for the Touring Office of the Canada Council and, in 1976, he was logistical coordinator for the Cultural Festival of the Montreal Olympics. Oscapella also performed as a concert pianist before his extensive administrative experiences.

p. 81   ... I make the company work then leave ... the reality of the financial situation...
Edward Oscapella, 1992.

p. 81   ... enable the restructuring of the company... [Grants were to continue not as operating grants but as project grants, allowing the councils to assess the company's ability to recover from its crisis. Neither council increased support and the company

was given a six month grace period to restructure. The Canada Council identified the three major factors that had inhibited a financial turnaround: the decline in earned revenues as a percentage of the budget, an inability to meet fund-raising objectives, and an increase in the operating budget due partially to the increasing cost of carrying a large deficit and the cost of the building. Strict stipulations for the project grants included: the hiring of an experienced manager who had the authority to hire and release staff, a fund-raising campaign to be launched within six months, documentation showing an outline of financial management controls and authority, a revised year's budget for 1981–82 indicating grant levels already confirmed, and a four month statement indicating actual revenue and expenses.]
Letter to TDT Board 1981, TDT Archives.

p. 81   ... Responding to the layoffs....
"Ballet Dancers Chip in to Help TDT Colleagues," *The Globe and Mail*, 23 November 1981, p. 19.

p. 81   ... Ed represented ... I'm going to make you pay attention....
Denis Joffre, 1998.

February 1982, performances continued only in their own small Winchester Street Theatre ... in 1982, the company held six performances at the studio theatre, and performed in New York State, Montreal, Hamilton, Ottawa, and at the Solar Stage lunchtime theatre in Toronto.

p. 82   ... I had this idea we should do a fund-raising thing....
David Earle, 1992.

p. 82   ... the best years. My poor darling brother....
Trish Beatty, 1998.

p. 82   ... There was tension, the whole building was on tenterhooks....
Karen duPlessis, 1998.

p. 82   ... Often, David had to mediate....
Trish Beatty, 1998.

p. 83   ... In the 1970s, the company helped trigger...
Michael Crabb, "Bodies with soul" *Maclean's*, November 29 1993.

p. 83   ... It's taken me fifteen years to work my way down....
Paula Citron, "A Step Back to Move Forward: Transition at Toronto Dance Theatre," *Performing Arts in Canada*, August 1983: 15–18.

Under Oscapella's management, the deficit was reduced from $281,809 in August 1981, to $202,088 by 31 August 1982, and $189,972 by 31 August 1983.

Although there was some coming and going of company members, dancers at this time (1981–83) were Merle Holloman, Charles Flanders, Suzette Sherman, Christopher House, Sherry Lanier, Grace Miyagawa, Karen duPlessis, Lucie Boissonot, Michael Conway, Monica George, Luc Tremblay, Julian Littleford, Sara Pettitt, Miguel Moore.

A Pearl at Any Price: 1983–1987

p. 84   ... they had been my teachers.... When I arrived as a director....
Kenny Pearl, 1998.

p. 85   ... how could these very choreographers have identical expectations? ...
Kenny Pearl, 1998.

p. 85   ... I think when Kenny came on he saw the potential of the company....
Christopher House, 1998.

Ellen Busby had been hired as a stage manager in 1979. She operated as a liaison between the artistic directors and Roger Jones when the communication between them had broken down. She was promoted to assistant general manager in 1981. She developed administration skills on the job and by attending the administration course held at the Banff Centre for the Arts.

p. 86   ... from my end as Manager....
Ellen Busby, 1992.

p. 87   ... Kenny was hired to be an agent for the four resident choreographers....
Paula Citron, "Toronto Dance Theatre Co-Founders Take Control," *The Toronto Star*, 20 September 1987, p. E7.

p. 87   ... During the four years I was at TDT ... it was never my company....
Kenny Pearl, 1998.

p. 88   ... after the "wildly successful" Mexican tour....
Kenny Pearl, 1998.

Creating the Work: Four

p. 88   ... My part involved roaring out of the wings, into a space within the group....
Karen duPlessis, written for TDT photo exhibit at the IDA Gallery, York University, 16–21 March 1998.

p. 89   ... Inspired by the frenetic pace of animated films....
William Littler, *The Toronto Star*, 29 October 1993.

p. 89   ... *Glass Houses* showed Mr. House at his most exciting....
Anna Kisselgoff, "Dance: Toronto Troupe in Brooklyn," *New York Times*, 22 April 1985, p. C14.

p. 90   ... I love women and this dance was a gift to one particular woman....
Peter Randazzo in the 25th Anniversary Programme, TDT Archives.

p. 90   ... didn't think I had a problem... I thought I was losing my mind....
Peter Randazzo, 1998.

p. 90   ... The forties are tricky for a dancer....
Sandy Naiman, "Still Some Dance in Me," *The Toronto Sun*, 19 September 1983, p. 37.

p. 90   ... Trish went through a huge transition coming to terms....
Suzette Sherman, 1980.

p. 91   ... I was going through a complete emotional, spiritual and physical....
Trish Beatty, 1998.

p. 92   ... a future of peace and world union...
dedication in *Painters and the Dance* programme, 22 September 1983, p. 14, TDT Archives.

p. 92   ... Originally, Patricia Beatty hired me just to dance in *Seastill*....
Holly Small, written for TDT photo exhibit at the IDA Gallery, York University, 16–28 March 1998.

p. 94 ... *Court of Miracles* ended with a beautiful tableau....
Penny Olorenshaw, written for TDT photo exhibit at the IDA
Gallery, York University, 16–28 March 1998.

p. 94 ... getting to be the little sheep....
Karen duPlessis, 1998.

p. 94 ... In spite of dancer poverty....
David Earle, 1998.

p. 96 ... the tears running down their faces....
Karen duPlessis, 1998.

p. 96 ... we had eight curtain calls....
Michael Trent, 1998.

p. 96 ... I think *Sacra* should represent a kind of triumph....
The Dancemakers "*Sacra Conversazione*" 1987, Moze Mossanen
producer.

Chapter Five

p. 99 ... I always figured this reunion would take place sooner or
later....
Kenny Pearl, 1998,

David Earle: 1987–1993

p. 99 ... Inevitable the creator....
Kenny Pearl, 1998,

p. 99 ... I've always been the moveable piece....
Paula Citron, "Toronto Dance Theatre Co Founders Take Control," *The Toronto Star*, 20 September 1987, p. E7.

An Englishman, Ken Peirson arrived in Canada in the 1960s. After working for the Ontario provincial government, he became the administrator of the Lois Smith School of Dance for six years. He joined Dancemakers in 1979, where he learned, on the job, to be an arts administrator. He took courses that dealt with arts organizations, grants, and fund-raising. In 1980, he attended the three-week arts administration course at the Banff Centre for the Arts. In 1982, Peirson left Dancemakers to manage the Green Thumb Theatre in Vancouver until 1985. He was the manager for the first year of Ballet British Columbia before returning to Toronto to manage the Skylight Theatre in the summer of 1987.

p. 100 ... there are different kinds of leadership....
Ken Peirson, 1992.

p. 100 ... it was like having the carpet pulled....
David Earle, 1992.

p. 101 ... He understood superbly the role of the artist....
Trish Beatty, 1998.

Golden Boys and Golden Girls

p. 102 ... We had been dancing together for so many years....
Suzette Sherman, 1998.

p. 102 ... experiment her heart out...
Coralee McLaren, 1998

p. 102 ... we were like a family unit....
Rosemary James, 1998.

p. 102   ... For twenty years we have been making love to Toronto....
Deirdre Kelly, "Toronto Dance Theatre," *Dance In Canada*,
Spring 1989: 21–25.

Company dancers in 1987 were: Grace Miyagawa, Merle Holloman,
Christopher House, Learie McNicolls, Karen duPlessis, Suzette
Sherman, Benoît Lachambre, Almond Small, Sylvie Bouchard, Laurence
Lemieux, William Elias, Ron Ladd, Michael Sean Marye, Rosemary
James, apprentice Miriane Braaf.

Creating the Works: Five

p. 103   ... One day it occurred to me....
David Earle, programme note, 1987, TDT Archives.

p. 105   ... although Artemis was the Greek goddess of the hunt....
Jack Anderson, *New York Times*, 2 December 1993.

Shooting from the Hip

p. 107   ... Heavy Artillery from Toronto... the splendid works on
view...
Anna Kisselgoff. "Some Heavy Artillery From Toronto," *New
York Times*, 14 November 1991: C. 15.

p. 107   ... Send the kiddies....
Janice Berman, "Exhilarating Diversity," *New York Newsday*,
15 November 1991, p. 11.

p. 108   ... 15 was one of the most challenging pieces I've ever done....
Graham McKelvie, written for TDT photo exhibit at the IDA
Gallery, York University, 16–21 March 1998.

In 1997, members of the original cast went to Vancouver to teach
Kudelka's choreography to Ballet BC. This is noteworthy because many
modern dance works do not translate well on a ballet company.

Lesser Value?

"arm's length" refers to maintaining a distance between the government
and the funding agency so the government cannot impose its views on
the funding agency or dictate the type of art that is being funded.

p. 110   ... today we are seeing those kinds of problems emerge
again....
Letter to Clifford Beatty, president of TDT Board, from Michel
Lemay, co-acting head of the Dance Section, Canada Council,
27 June 1991, TDT Archives.

p. 111   ... my understanding of an artist....
Trish Beatty, 1998.

p. 111   ... I was torn in two....
Trish Beatty, 1998.

Creating the Works: Six

p. 112   ... The piece came alive for me at the middle when Sean
Marye....
Robert Everett Green, *The Globe and Mail*, 12 November 1992.

p. 112   ... David couldn't tell me....
Trish Beatty, 1998.

p. 113   ... Bookers don't like me....
Paula Citron, "Dance Pioneer's Farewell Celebrates Lifeforce,"
The Toronto Star, 21 February 1992.

p. 114   ... Beatty being Beatty....
William Littler, "Beatty's Last New Piece Speaks of Deep Feelings," *The Toronto Star*, 26 February 1992, p. F4.

p. 114   ... A disturbing piece....
William Littler, 26 February 1992, p. F4.

p. 115   ... I realized it was a piece about many people like me....
Francis Mason, "A Conversation with Christopher House," *Canadian Dance Studies 2 1997*, edited by Selma Odom and Mary Jane Warner, Graduate Programme in Dance, York University, p. 110.

p. 115   ... I have a great affinity for *Early Departures*....
Michael Trent, 1998.

Company dancers for 1991 were: Kate Alton, Miriane Braaf, Monica Burr, Bill Coleman, Pascal Desrosiers, Christopher House, Susanna Hood, Rosemary James, Laurence Lemieux, Graham McKelvie, David Pressault, Michael Sean Marye, Coralee McLaren, Suzette Sherman, Michael Trent.

The Twenty-Fifth Anniversary

p. 116   ... the idea — a good one
Robert Everett-Green, "Still Strong After All These Years," *The Globe and Mail*, 5 November 1993.

p. 116   ... This language.... Suzette has been the woman in my life....
1993, 25th Anniversary Programme, TDT Archives.

p. 119   ... David Earle stood on the stage of the Premiere Dance Theatre....
Robert Everett-Green, 5 November 1993.

p. 119   ... with over a month to go....
cited in 1993, 25th Anniversary Programme, TDT Archives.

Company dancers were: Christopher House, Kate Alton, Miriane Braaf, Bill Coleman, Pascal Desrosiers, Karen duPlessis, Susanna Hood, Laurence Lemieux, Sean Marye, Graham McKelvie, Coralee McLaren, Learie McNicolls, Naoko Murakoshi, Marie Josée Dubois, Megan Hayes, Sasha Ivanochko, Suzette Sherman, Ron Stewart, Michael Trent, Stephan Beckon, and apprentices, Kirsten Andersen and Todd Durling.

Next in Line

p. 120   ... I think from the time Kenny....
Christopher House, 1998.

Chapter Six

p. 121   ... we trained him and encouraged him...
Peter Randazzo, 1998.

Christopher House 1994–

p. 121   ... Newfoundland at that time was so dark....
Christopher House, 1998

p. 122   ... experience had been with Graham technique....
Christopher House, 1998.

p. 122   ... I found her very inspiring ... I decided to become a dancer....
Christopher House, 1998.

p. 122   ... I was starving....
Christopher House, 1998.

p. 123   ... I guess we are four....
Deirdre Kelly, "Toronto Dance Theatre," *Dance in Canada*,
Spring 1989: 21.

p. 123   ... I didn't feel I needed to be compensated because I felt the
opportunity itself was pretty special....
Christopher House, 1998.

p. 124   ... I am a dancer and choreographer ...
manifesto provided by Christopher House, 1998.

The New Partner

Jini Stolk came to TDT with a significant understanding of the Toronto
arts community. Prior to 1994, she had been the executive director of
the Toronto Theatre Alliance. This position gave her a unique perspective on TDT's reputation. She had watched the company through its
crises and successes of the eighties. She recognized the artistic accomplishments of the company, but she also had heard of their financial
difficulties.

p. 126   ... Jini stated....
Jini Stolk, 1998.

p. 126   ... are volunteers....
Christopher House, 1998.

p. 126   ... the value of an institution....
Christopher House, 1998.

"Time to Go"

p. 127   ... from my side, it was time....
Denis Joffre, 1998.

p. 128   ... it was like people smiled at us when we said something....
Trish Beatty, 1998.

p. 128   ... I believe it is time to take steps to preserve....
David Earle, 1998.

p. 128   ... We can't complain about what Christopher is doing...
Peter Randazzo, 1998.

p. 128   ... It's not what happened it's how it happened....
Trish Beatty, 1998.

Opening the Windows

p. 128   ... is more than just a fancy rehearsal hall....
Ron Snippe, 1998.

p. 129   ... I've always been unable to tell what Christopher....
Michael Trent, 1998.

Creating the Works: Seven

p. 130   ... using her legs like compass points....
Amanda Gibbs, *Dance International*, Summer 1998: 19.

p. 132   ... the audience response was mysterious...
Naoko Murakoshi, "The Blending of Cultures: Dance Canada
1994 Performs to Sold-Out Tokyo Crowds," *The Canada-Japan
Business Review*, April–May 1995.

Company dancers in 1997 were Kirsten Andersen, Darrin Bonin, Bill Coleman, Marie-Josée Dubois, Sasha Ivanochko, Laurence Lemieux, Sean Marye, Graham McKelvie, Naoko Murakoshi, James Robertson, Sonya Stefan, Ron Stewart, Michael Trent, and Laura West.

Return to the Heartland

p. 132   ... It is a church, my family helped build this....
Trish Beatty, 1998.

p. 133   ... *Dancing the Goddess* was conceived....
Terrill Maguire, 1998.

p. 133   ... "Suzette is somebody who is extremely important....
Michael Trent, 1998.

p. 134   ... such a distinctive page of our choreographic past....
William Littler, "Taking Passion Literally," *The Toronto Star*, 5 February 1998, p. A31.

p. 134   ... David Trish and I are survivors....
Peter Randazzo, 1992, 1998.

p. 134   ... Bill had come to Canada....
David Earle, 1998.

p. 135   ... life affirming....
Christopher House, manifesto, 1985.

p. 135   ... in the heart of myself....
Peggy Baker, 1998.

Chapter Seven

Quotes for this chapter were taken from interviews and conversations between May and August 1998. Those not taken from this period are noted.

Dance Can Suggest a Whole Life Process

p. 137   ... Dance can suggest a whole life process....
Francis Mason, "A Conversation with Christopher House," *Canadian Dance Studies 2 1997*, edited by Selma Odom and Mary Jane Warner, Graduate Programme in Dance, York University, p. 110.

On Teaching

p. 138   ... Right from my first year....
Paula Citron, "Talking With Susan Macpherson," *Dance In Canada*, Summer 1986: 22.

On Choreography

p. 142   ... *The Miserere*....
Luc Tremblay, written for TDT photo exhibit at the IDA Gallery York University, 16–21 March 1998.

p. 143   ... most vivid recollection ...
Luc Tremblay written for TDT photo exhibit at the IDA Gallery York University, 16–21 March 1998.

p. 145   ... the dancers inspire me...
Francis Mason, "A Conversation with Christopher House" *Canadian Dance Studies 2 1997*, ed. Odom, Selma and Warner, Mary Jane, Graduate Programme in Dance, York University, p. 97.

On Critics

p. 146   ... In dance criticism...
Patricia Beatty, *Form Without Formula,* Toronto: Press of Terpsichore Ltd., 1989, p. 57.

On Dancing

p. 145   ... when I'm dancing Trish's works....
Paula Citron, "Four Choreographers Keep Dancer on Toes," *The Toronto Star*, 16 January 1987, p. D7.

On Ricardo Abreut the "Silent Partner"

p. 147   ... Ricardo Abreut had a deep, lifelong devotion....
from Tribute to Ricardo, 1995, posted in the lobby of TDT.

Last Words

p. 153   ... do you have to audition....
David Earle, 1992.

p. 153   ... it is well-known that the hot house life....
written for TDT 1998 *Newsletter*.

Selected Bibliography

This is a list of books cited in the text, as well as those consulted in its preparation.

Full bibliographical information for articles found in archival collections or in journals, newspapers, and/or periodicals are provided in the appropriate endnotes. Interviews are also cited in the endnotes. For a comprehensive list of those interviewed, please see Acknowledgements.

Anderson, Carol. *This Passion*. Toronto: Dance Collection Danse, 1998.

Beatty, Patricia. *Form Without Formula: A Concise Guide to the Choreographic Process*. Toronto: Press of Terpsichore Ltd., 1989.

Campbell, Nora Baird, ed. *Dance Manager's Handbook*. Toronto: Dance In Canada Association, 1986.

Canada Council. *The Canada Council and its Programs*. Ottawa: The Canada Council, 1971–1990.

———. *Annual Reports*. Ottawa: Canada Council, 1971–1990.

Cohan, Robert. *The Dance Workshop*. New York: Simon & Schuster, 1986.

Crean, Susan. *Who's Afraid of Canadian Culture?* Don Mills, Ontario: General Publishing, 1976.

De Mille, Agnes. *Martha: The Life And Works Of Martha Graham*. New York: Random House, 1991.

Fulford, Robert. *An Introduction to the Arts in Canada*. Toronto: Copp Clark in association with the Citizenship Branch, Department of the Secretary of State of Canada, and Publishing Centre, Supply and Services Canada, 1977.

Jackson, Graham. *Dance as Dance: Selected Reviews and Essays*. Scarborough, Ontario: Catalyst, 1978.

———. "Martha's Web: Ten Years with Toronto Dance Theatre." *Dance in Canada*, Winter 1978–79: 3–8.

Jowitt, Deborah. *Time and the Dancing Image*. Los Angeles: University of California Press, 1988.

MacSkimming, Roy. *For Arts Sake: A History of the Ontario Arts Council 1963–1983*. Toronto: Ontario Arts Council, 1983.

McKinsey and Co. Inc. *Directions for the Dance in Canada*. Ottawa: Canada Council Information Services, April 1973.

Neufeld, James. *The Power to Rise*, Toronto: University of Toronto Press, 1996.

Odom, Selma and Mary Jane Warner, eds. *Canadian Dance Studies: 1 & 2*, Toronto: Graduate Programme in Dance, York University. 1994, 1997.

Officer, Jillian. *Works Which Have Appeared in the Repertoire of The Toronto Dance Theatre.* Unpublished list, University of Waterloo, 1981.

———, ed. *The Encyclopedia of Theatre Dance in Canada.* Toronto: Dance Collection Danse, 1989.

Oxenham, Andrew and Michael Crabb. *Dance Today in Canada.* Toronto: Simon and Pierre, 1976.

Pasquill, Frank and Joan Horsman. *Wooden Pennies: A Report on Cultural Funding Patterns in Canada.* Toronto: York University Press, 1973.

Plumptre, Timothy. *Simply Dance: Inside Canadian Professional Dance.* Ottawa: Department of Communications, 1982.

Saxton, Nadine. *Toronto Dance Theatre: An Example of Arts Administration in Canada.* Unpublished thesis. York University, 1993.

Wyman, Max. *Dance Canada.* Vancouver: Douglas and McIntyre Ltd., 1989.

Index

The founders and then later Christopher House appear on almost every page of this book, for this reason, they were not indexed.